CW00759022

EMPOWER YOUR DIVINE SELF IN

The Contentment Dividend

★ STARRED REVIEW "A valuable guide that can be read repeatedly ...
on finding a unique, ongoing way of quieting the mind's chatter and
accessing the higher self." —*BlueInk Review* **Notable Book**

"Encouraging seekers toward union with the divine and experiences
of awe, wonder, and love, *The Contentment Dividend* is a compelling,
supportive spiritual guide." —*Foreword* **Clarion Review**

"Throughout, Goddart makes the case in clear, inviting prose that
we need to become attached to something higher within ourselves
and pursue spiritual purpose. With many, varied meditations on
everyday life and situations, the book will prove a valuable compen-
dium of thought-provoking and spiritual reflections for readers who
strive to better themselves through meditation and spiritual growth."
—*BookLife* by *Publishers Weekly*

★ IR APPROVED "Through a tapestry of intimate spiritual reflections,
The Contentment Dividend guides truth-seekers to penetrate surface
identities, embrace life's secret curriculum, and reunite with the luminous core of divine being. ... the author shines in addressing existential quandaries of purpose, resistance, and self-transformation. ...
For spiritual voyagers fatigued by surface living, this real-world monk
offers welcome perspective and wings." —*IndieReader*

"*The Contentment Dividend* is a book of meditations told in a story-like
format that will allow readers to dive deep into a practice for self-realization and self-discovery. Each meditation teaches readers to think

deeper than before because life is much more than what we see in our physical lives. With themes of faith, gratitude, acceptance, perception, intention, and manifestation, this book, based on the Ancient Word of God, will help readers cultivate a daily spiritual practice." —**Kristi Elizabeth,** *Los Angeles Book Review*

"*The Contentment Dividend* is an original and worthy guide to navigating the many pitfalls, twists and turns on the spiritual path. With humor, tact, and reassuring wisdom Goddart has provided a **Light**-filled path out of the seeming abyss of our modern materialistic lifestyles. This Light is available to all who seek it with grace and humility, and those who bask in its radiance are not only transformed but empowered to change the world." —**Andrew Vidich, PhD,** author of *Love is a Secret: The Mystic Quest for Divine Love* and *Light Upon Light: Five Master Paths to Awaken the Mindful Self*

"It has been an honor, privilege, and joy to pour over Michael Goddart's brilliant, poetic, and divine combination of words. For those seekers looking to identify and embrace a spiritual journey to realize their true self, The Contentment Divide can lead the way. You'll be riveted by the 49 intuited meditations, taking you on a joyous experience." —**Janice Fletcher, EdD,** author of *Wisdom from the Inner Teacher*

"As we might expect from a deeply spiritual man who has been meditating since he was very young, Michael Goddart has produced an intimate memoir of his lifelong spiritual journey in the form of a series of ever deeper meditations. He writes beautifully, and every short piece in *The Contentment Dividend* is laden with fresh insights that make you want to read them all with a pencil in your hand and a pad of paper nearby. This is a book especially written for people who have been disappointed by the ultimate spiritual shallowness of modern Christianity, and who find themselves in the second half of their lives without a satisfying spiritual home and still seeking. In Michael Goddart's long-practiced synthesis of Eastern and Western thought, many such seekers will again find balance. As Michael says, 'During this life, we are saddled with a mad, ruling mind, riffing off a welter of desires and thoughts that prevent us from attaining true, lasting happiness.' And, 'Our soul is our true being of consciousness, free of mind and body, whose one constant longing is to return to our true Home, an infinite sweet surging sea of pure, eternal love. That's not a mythical misconception. It is our heritage.'" —**Roberta Grimes,** author of *The Fun of Dying* and *Liberating Jesus*

"With an authentic and inviting voice, Goddart takes the reader's hand and gently guides them through beautiful reflections on life, death, and opening to the divine. Seekers new and experienced alike will discover a deeper connection to their own truth by savoring the kindhearted, wise, and poignant contemplations that Goddart distills from his life experiences." —**Patrick Paul Garlinger,** author of *Endless Awakening: Time, Paradox, and the Path to Enlightenment*

"Goddart, a well-traveled and experienced spiritual writer, shares 49 essays on the heady subjects of personal enlightenment, reunion with God, and the provisional nature of the physical. ... they recall small reflecting ponds with yawning depths." —*Kirkus Reviews*

"As the host of my own podcast, *Tell Me Your Story,* I can attest to the importance in everyone's life of meditation. It is as essential as the air we breathe, the water we drink, the sleep we take in order for us to stay connected to the divine. This book provides people with an opportunity to add a new dimension to their lives. It is an inspiration to me. It's how to keep my balance in life and I hope you will avail yourself of this opportunity." —**Richard Dugan,** Video Producer

"More so than most spiritual and self-help guides, … readers interested in books centered on growth and empowerment … will find *The Contentment Dividend* an uplifting, fine discussion of the opportunities present in daily living for those who would contemplate the deeper roots and meaning of contentment." —**D. Donovan,** Senior Reviewer, *Midwest Book Review*

A New Now

Winner of the Nautilus Book Award
Winner of the Living Now Book Award
Winner of the Indie Reader Discovery Award
Winner of the National Indie Excellence Award
Winner of the Independent Publisher Book Award
Winner of the American Book Fest Best Book Award
Honoree of the Eric Hoffer Book Award
Finalist for the Next Generation Indie Book Awards
Finalist for the Foreword Indies Book of the Year Award

"Goddart's guide instructs readers in the cultivation of spiritual growth and connecting to the 'infinite, inexhaustible aquifer' of divine knowledge the author argues lies in each of us. Goddart claims that by developing this wisdom we can live each moment fully, always working toward a unique, self-determined purpose in life. Goddart's relationship with the reader emerges as the true strength of the book. . . . he acts as a warm, welcoming guide. . . . Great for fans of Eckhart Tolle's *The Power of Now*" —*BookLife* by *Publishers Weekly*

★ IR APPROVED "Michael Goddart's A NEW NOW is a timely, enlightened and well-researched guide that provides concrete tips for focusing energy, enriching relationships as well as enhancing creativity and productivity." —*IndieReader*

"*A New Now*. . . surveys virtually the entire range of daily life and activity and provides key insights to help people navigate the issues they are facing in their lives. . . . countless areas present positive ways

to make a difference in the way one feels, thinks, and interacts. . . . "
—**Santosh Krinsky**, President, New Leaf Distributing Company

"*A New Now* is filled to the brim with very helpful advice about how one can better navigate the twists and turns that invariably arise in one's day-to-day life . . . one can feel the author's guiding presence throughout the text which is both warm and encouraging." —**David Christopher Lane, PhD**, Professor Of Philosophy, Mt. San Antonio College, Founder of the MSAC Philosophy Group

"*A New Now* really is an instruction book for how to think about— and fix—your experience of life." —**Toby Johnson**, author of *Finding Your Own True Myth: What I Learned from Joseph Campbell*

"*A New Now* gives self-help spirituality readers an empowering approach to awakening their higher consciousness . . . nuggets of insights along with clear, practical, and inspiring guidance direct readers on how to achieve both wisdom and equilibrium." —**D. Donovan**, *Midwest Book Review*

"*A New Now* delivers on its promise to guide the reader through the thought-maze of mind to mindfulness; unpleasant psychological states to equipoise; spiritual darkness to the experience of one's soul in the Now. Goddart's guiding voice throughout is both wisdom-filled and profoundly practical. . . ." —**Eliot Jay Rosen,** author of *Experiencing the Soul—Before Birth, During Life, After Death*

"A potentially life changing, life enhancing read, A New Now is an exceptionally insightful and motivating instructional guide and manual that is especially and unreservedly recommended. . . ." —**Small Press Bookwatch**, *Midwest Book Review*

TAKE THE MOST FASCINATING JOURNEY

In Search of Lost Lives

Winner of the Living Now Book Award
Winner of the Body Mind Spirit Book Award
Winner of the National Indie Excellence Award
Winner of the American Book Fest Best Book Award

"*In Search of Lost Lives* is a brilliant exploration of a soul's journey through many past lives. Imagine how different our lives and our world would be if more of us had access to this kind of knowledge. Michael Goddart has given us an invaluable gift." —**Raymond A. Moody, Jr., MD, PhD,** author of *Life After Life*

"…a veritable epic of reincarnation literature … fans of reincarnation literature will find Goddart's account both fascinating and ambitious, an attempt to map the entire tangled biography of one spirit. There's a good deal of vibrancy in Goddart's piece-by-piece tapestry of his extended personal past, particularly in its free-flowing treatment of concepts that are typically fixed in accounts like this, such as gender and particularly sexuality…" —*Kirkus Reviews*

"Pythagoras is said to have recalled all of his former lives but unlike Michael Goddart he left no record for us to examine. In Search of Lost Lives, Goddart's sweeping narrative, allows us to contemplate a journey through thousands of lives in the quest for complete spiritual liberation—which makes this book a significant and timely contribution to an exciting and important field." —**James O'Dea**, Former President of the Institute of Noetic Sciences, author, activist and mystic

DISCOVER THE INSPIRATION IN

Spiritual Revolution

Winner—Best Spirituality/Self-Help Book
of the Hollywood Spiritual Film and Entertainment Festival

"A book of true wisdom. Save yourself pain and read it." —**Bernie Siegel, MD,** *Love, Medicine & Miracles*

"A clear vision of the spiritual path. It will prove valuable to anyone, regardless of their religion or creed. This book shines with compassion and simplicity, which are what the most majestic spiritual visions have always embodied." —**Larry Dossey, MD,** *Prayer Is Good Medicine*

"*Spiritual Revolution* is filled with spiritual nuggets that will nourish your soul." —**Gerald G. Jampolsky, MD,** *Love Is Letting Go of Fear*

"*Spiritual Revolution* is a powerful book that puts you in touch with your own soul." —**Lynn Andrews,** *Medicine Woman*

"*Spiritual Revolution* glows with wisdom and heart. Every page is a nugget of inspiration, sure to bring your soul home to peace and clarity. I love it!" —**Alan Cohen,** *A Deep Breath of Life*

"...an open-hearted expression of the highest principles and ideals from the Eastern spiritual traditions." —**Dan Millman,** *The Laws of Spirit*

The Contentment Dividend

Also by Michael Goddart

A New Now: Your Guide to Mastering Wisdom Daily,
Achieving Equilibrium, and Empowering Your Nobler Self

In Search of Lost Lives: Desire, Sanskaras, and the
Evolution of a Mind&Soul

BLISS: 33 Simple Ways to Awaken Further

Spiritual Revolution: A Seeker's Guide;
52 Powerful Principles for Your Mind & Soul

The Contentment Dividend

MEDITATIONS FOR REALIZING YOUR TRUE SELF

Michael Goddart

Clear Path Press
Rhinebeck, New York

The Contentment Dividend: Meditations for Realizing Your True Self Copyright © 2023 by Michael Goddart

All rights reserved. No part of this book may be used or reproduced in any manner without the consent of the author except in critical articles or reviews. Contact the publisher for information.

Paperback ISBN 978-1-960090-42-3
Hardcover ISBN 978-1-960090-41-6
eBook ISBN 978-1-960090-43-0

Library of Congress Control Number 2023922318

Book design by Colin Rolfe
Cover photograph by Sami Sert

Distributed by Epigraph Books

Clear Path Press
c/o Epigraph Books
22 East Market Street, Suite 304
Rhinebeck, New York 12572
(845) 876-4861
epigraphps.com

Listen, dear friend,

You are doing your best to live

this life you have been given.

Beyond your fondest imaginings,

the most wondrous life awaits you.

Let us explore the way to it together.

Contents

Author's Note

You have the power within you to liberate your soul from the mind's dominance and achieve reunion with God. The forty-nine intuited meditations take you on *this journey* of discovery of realizing your true spiritual self, understanding the immortal truths of existence, and how to focus your mind and life to achieve daily—and ultimately consummate—contentment.

Some of the names of the meditations may sound obscure, cryptic, even fanciful. Let them pique your curiosity. May the discussion enable you to open to and comprehend the teachings of realized Masters and true Saints. These are the fully God-realized humans who come to awaken us to our unlimited spiritual potential. By engaging with the meditations, you will undergo a revolution in how you navigate life's challenges, accessing the wisdom of your higher mind and your soul's yearning to further your spiritual evolution.

This is your opportunity to embrace and engage in a New Reckoning. When you find yourself in a sweet, quiet moment, ask yourself:

What has my life meant to me thus far?

Am I interested in evolving spiritually and can I embrace that?

To what extent am I open to experiencing a revolution in the way I understand and relate to my mind, soul, and journey through existence?

Return to these questions when the spirit moves you. This is your chance to see and enjoy life and spirituality in a new light—or rather, a light that has been within you all the time.

Honor your curiosity and turn the page to engage with the thrilling meaning of life—yours in particular—and your call to inner adventure.

1   The Inescapable Unknown

The inescapable unknown—we all face it. Regardless of how unaware we are of it. In those unexpected moments when we come face-to-face with it—waking in the middle of the night; realizing we are going to die; not knowing what is coming— we may feel gripped by fear. We may feel anxious, apprehensive, leery of life. Rather than embrace our fear of the unknown and get to the nub of it, our mind will seek avoidance. At any hint of a confrontation with the unknown, we likely turn away to fill ourselves with what we know—people, work, familiar sensations (why are the re-welcoming allurements of drinking, smoking, and getting high so comforting?), food, sex, music, games, shows, *sleep*. It is much nicer to sleep and sleep-walk through life than to face the unknown.

It is more gratifying, at least superficially, to stuff ourselves with what feels familiar, even if it's traveling to three new unknown places each year. The planning for the trip, the travel, the new place to see, and the reliving of the trip conceals the unknown we keep at bay.

To begin to accept the unknown is to embrace life as it is now, being present in the now, the raw present. No buffers. No boundaries. We may harbor ideas of what's coming and these may provide anticipation or anxiety, but these too remove us from being in the unknown. The unknown is inescapable, but we do our best to escape it.

News masquerades as the unknown becoming known. But if you've ever studied the home page of a major newspaper, you'll realize that most of the articles are conjecture. They are opinions about what can happen. There is a certain gratification and, for some, a feeling of safety and familiarity in keeping up with and taking in "what's happening." This provides a sense of control, of grounding, of purported reality, of knowing—all of which banish the true unknown. For those, especially older people, who might allow themselves to dwell for a moment or longer on death, they may realize that they really don't know what will lead up to it. Will you be immobilized by a stroke? Will dementia inexorably make you lose your grip? Will you waste away in a nursing home?

Those who believe in a continuing consciousness after the cessation of this physical life may be attached to particular ideas about it: seeing a great Saint, being reunited with family, seeing and being with other loved ones who have passed on, floating in a sanctified sea of bliss, having fantasy after fantasy fulfilled. But the truth is, the experiences that await you after your passing are still *unknown*.

The unknown is the inescapable fact of existence—unless you are omniscient.

To detach mentally and strip away everything from your life is to begin to commune with the true self. Not the self that is defined by work or family, achievements or failures, or favored recreations. But the self that can expand into ineffable knowing. We each have a self that is typically buried under the onrush of the day's demands and the lure of the night's escapes. This self of ours can be cultivated and can become known, experience by experience. We are so habitually dominated by our demanding thoughts and urges that it remains elusive. But our true self is always waiting for us.

2   Unsparing Kindness

If we truly knew how people suffer—physically, emotionally, mentally, spiritually—it would transform the way we treat others. We are each suffering through the rigors of living from the time we are born until we die. If we could fully know the suffering of each person with whom we interact, it would induce empathy and, with that, we could express unsparing kindness.

We were born to grow in love. Getting through each day, we even suffer unknowingly. Our soul is a spark of the divine, longing to return to God. The demands of our mind and our existence in this world mask that separation. We are trying to meet the necessities and the desires of our mind while our true essence is love. Existing in a realized state of love—that is the journey that beckons. Our soul, the eternal beingness that keeps us alive, is a projection of God. Our journey through this lifetime could be a journey to LoveSource, another name for God.

Day after day we come in contact physically, as well as mentally, with people and animals and other living beings.

When meeting the people—strangers, store staff, coworkers, hired workers, health professionals and other professionals, friends, frenemies, relatives, family, prospective partners— many of us act under the sway of ego in a state of yet-to-be realized love. Each of these physical and mental contacts is an opportunity to think, speak, and act with unsparing kindness. Be aware of each interaction and give your kindness unstintingly.

In many surveys, when asked what quality the person would most want in a partner, the overwhelming response is kindness.

Knowing yourself and others to some extent, it is easy to get hurt, to feel unsure, unseen, unheard—to feel like a lone cactus on a sandy dune, longing for the dew drops of a balmy night. This is one reason why it is vital to give unsparing kindness—it acts as a sweet balm on the other person and on you. By giving kindness unsparingly, you raise the energetic love of self and others in both you and the person to whom you are extending kindness. You are giving but also receiving much more than you may be aware of. You are cultivating and realizing yourself, your truer self. Being human in this way pays dividends that beget dividends of content. The content is love. And that is the only content that continues to exist beyond time. Giving selflessly, unsparingly of kindness mystically fills you and transmutes you to a higher state of being. You are transformed in an ineffable, auspicious contentment.

What is the fate of being unsparingly kind? You pray it forward. Your kindness goes out in the world as an inducement to empower ourselves to transcend our down-pulling world and minds. Through others' experience of your kindness, you inspire them to pray it forward.

Ruled in various ways and degrees by your ego most of the time, you shunt it aside in those timeless moments. If it rears up, voicing gratuitous judgments and criticisms as it is wont to do, overrule it. When you are selflessly, unstintingly kind, you imbibe yourself in saintliness. This is a wonderful fate to transmute into.

You also open yourself to being embraced by the pervading Oneness. One way the Oneness expresses is as the omni-loving force of kindness. What sweet balms may come when?

3   The Elusive Self

The elusive self remains hidden to most, yet it possesses accessible treasures. In stillness, it can rise to the fore of your awareness. But so easily is it lost, forgotten, trampled by the onrush of lazy, urgent thought. Some mistakenly believe they indulge their higher self by following the whims of the mind. A mistaken letting go to steep in sensual saturation can be the cult that some follow in the pursuit of the elusive self. But outer pleasures bury it. Looking outside yourself for gratification only serves to animate the restless mind, allowing the physical senses to dominate.

The mind wants more, then more, exerting itself to get what it wants; the self retreats further, imprisoned by your attending to outer transiencies. Rather than mistakenly letting go by following the mind's succumbing to physical senses, you can learn to allow the elusive self to reveal who you can be.

What is the self? The self is your spirit, the beingness of your soul and its expression of soul-like qualities in your higher mind and awareness. In this context, the elusive self means your higher self, which, when it is predominant, you experience its five main qualities. That is, you are present, centered, positive, peaceful, and content. You experience this self when you are being your most authentic you. The self is experienced on a continuum. That is because until you have mastered the mind and it is truly a handmaiden of the soul and you freely and wholly express the storehouse of virtues, the mind's waves of thoughts and impulses ruffle you and overtake your awareness.

The mind has ineluctable striking power and staying power. That is why when you sigh and feel peace, simply being present and content, unexpected worries and anguish barrel through to disturb and hijack you from your golden good moments.

You can always return to your spiritual center. You can learn what works best to return you to your stillness. In stillness, the elusive self can rise to the fore, offering a refuge of freedom and sweet yearning. So subtle in the stillness, can you experience when it pulses with love? Can you sense the all-pervasive Spirit and embrace your true self's yearning for union? If not, be still. The all-pervasive Spirit exudes a loving quiet and wants to bathe you in beingness—that is, a true letting go in which the busy mind falls away and you float in a spacious spiritual sea.

Allow your spiritual self to be, for it pulses with love. It offers a refuge of freedom—freedom from concern, worry, fear of impending doom. The real, true self offers a surety that you are going on; come what may you will be fine. Whatever you suffer, you *will* come through to the other end wiser, further along your experienced being. For if you cultivate awareness, you can learn to align with the self, allowing repose, so the elusive self unfurls and you begin to feel and savor true contentment.

The elusive self is revealed the more you collect your attention and withdraw from the world. Purely concentrated attention has great power. With it, you can be in an expansive sea of bliss, allowing higher and deeper states of contentment to lift you above the transient cares and troubles of this life.

This physical world is a great deception in which the elusive self is imprisoned. Nothing is lasting, nothing is real—yet we are meant to believe it, to chase after everything that excites our senses and mind. The booby prize: another life wasted and with it, the chance to realize and be the elusive self, the real you, and be one of the symphonies of soul.

4   Blinding Promises

You're going on a hike! You've been looking forward to it for two weeks. You've never been on this hike before, and you haven't seen your friend for weeks. There's so much to talk about! You arrive where you've agreed to meet five minutes early. You wait. After ten minutes, you text. No response. Probably rushing to get here, you think. Later, you text again. No response. You're a bit concerned—you hope they're okay. You call. No answer. You don't know what to do. Did they forget? You text again. Walk back and forth.

There's so much you wanted to share. While thinking about the outing, what you wanted to talk about, a text comes through—not today sorry I need a me morning.

That's it? You're frustrated, angry, bummed. You still want to talk. But you think, I'm taking off and I'm going to enjoy every moment of the hike. Hiking and talking was not meant to be. Later, enjoying the scrunch of your steps, the birdcalls, you think, doing the hike by myself is what I really need. Perhaps I'm being saved from negative energy. When you return to your car, you are feeling good.

That evening and throughout the week, you mull over

what happened, however. By the time you have let go of the little remaining frustration, you have gained clarity. In this and similar situations, you not only made an agreement with your friend, you also made a promise to yourself of how your hike was going to be: visualizing it, mentally repeating conversations. When the agreement did not play at all like your unwitting promise, you reacted negatively and became discontent. You sowed the field of your mind to reap discontent again and again whenever this incident arose in your mind. You blinded yourself to the reality that did arrive. Regardless of how wonderful or frustrating the experience might have been, it could not come to pass just as you envisioned it— with invigorating exercise, communing with nature, sharing your news. Unwitting blinding promises you make with yourself sow discontent.

The next week is a really tough one. You are exhausted, scattered, relieved the weekend is here. You have no plans this Friday. Why not make some me time for yourself, you ask. You deserve a reward. You plan the perfect evening. It will be an evening of indulgence with a luscious dinner plus dessert and great music, followed by a movie you've been wanting to see. You prepare the food, heat the oven, and midway to reaching the temperature, the power goes out. Surely, the power will come back in a few minutes. You wait. It doesn't. You can't believe it. You think of going out to eat and catching a movie somewhere that does have power, but then you realize the garage door won't open. You can't reach the release cord that hangs over your car in your old house. You're a captive. With the flashlight in your phone, *which is running out,* you find a few candles, finally a packet of matches, light the candles, power off the phone, which now you must carefully husband, and snack on chips and wonder how are you going to spend the evening.

With the evening you planned, precisely imagined, ardently embraced, and enthusiastically looked forward to, you made an iron-clad promise to yourself. Your vision blinded you to the fact that the actual *living* of this planned evening could not be your expected physical, emotional, mental experience. Subsuming the plan into your mental field as a false future reality, you sowed the field to reap discontent.

Rather than calling and/or checking the website of the power provider every twenty minutes, running down your phone's charge, letting yourself become exasperated and filling with discontent, you might have followed a feeling you then ignored to carry two candles through the room into the bathroom, where, following a feeling, you searched at the back of a lower cabinet for more candles you now remember you'd hidden away ages ago. Feeling it's worth a try, you run a bath, throw in bubble bath salts, and there's just enough hot water to get in, immerse yourself, and let go. Yes, this is the perfect way to de-stress you might have felt.

The next weeks, you meditate at times about these incidents and realize you had a choice about becoming discontent. You enjoy an epiphany—if that's the right word for it—that your mental disposition is about accepting the reality of the now. No agreement or plan you make with others or yourself is bound to be realized as you imagine it. Because you are not there living through it. They are projections of how you think and/or want your life to play out at the time you accept or embrace the agreement or plan. The will of the goddess is sweet. Has a higher purpose. You remember the saying: "Do your best and leave the rest." You aim to endeavor to do that.

The next month, a relative you're so, so fond of has a baby! A month early. You visit her, all excited. When you see your dear cousin (before you see the baby), she bursts into tears. Her baby has a critical congenital heart defect. Needs surgery within a year. After that, how many more surgeries the doctors don't know. You're devastated. She is disconsolate. But—

BABIES ARE INNOCENT. You sit on the bed, holding her hand. While you talk, you think, "Why did this happen? This beautiful, blameless baby, perfect in every way but born this way. And my cousin is such a good person." Your heart hurts. Life isn't fair. You feel so terribly sorry for her. Sorrier for the baby. It is so unfair.

Back home over the next few days, you feel frustrated. Disheartened. Discontent. At a loss. Life just doesn't make sense. In this world, there are so many injustices, inequities. Is life just a random biological lottery? You ponder this. At times you feel more frustration, hurt, deeper discontent, and sometimes curious.

You feel like you want to look for answers. You search online, starting with, "Why are babies born with birth defects?" On what looks like a reputable medical center's website, you read that defects "might be caused by genetics, infection, radiation, or drug exposure, or there might be no known reason." This does not help. You narrow your search and ask about critical congenital heart disease. On the website of the National Library of Medicine you find, "In most cases, the cause of CCHD is unknown. A variety of genetic and environmental factors likely contribute to this complex condition." This does not satisfy you.

There must be a real why—at least, in your heart of hearts you hope there is. Is life just haphazard? The saying (or is it a line from a poem) comes to you: "Ours is not to reason why, ours is but to do and die." Ye gods, ye goddesses! What a world. You go to bed, discombobulated.

The next morning you wake up and the word "karma" surfaces. You decide to explore this, maybe figure out if it's nonsense. You start with Wikipedia, your go-to online source of information, which you contribute to whenever you feel rewarded (and Wikipedia's ask gets to your conscience). What you read is intriguing. You read more articles and your curiosity awakens as you ponder this.

Over the next few days, you think about it. *Karma* (Sanskrit: action; cause and effect) is the only thing that makes sense. You reflect on your own life, remembering an unexpected inheritance from an aunt who had three children. You were surprised but also had the odd feeling that it was meant to be. Was this good karma you had earned? Reflecting more, you remember some special people who came into your life who felt inexplicably familiar. The first times you were with them you had a buzzy, uncanny feeling—as though you'd known them before. In other lives?

One morning you wake up and, lying in bed, it comes to you. A realization. You want to let go of yourself. But how?

Where? You feel limited in this boundary called "yourself." The next morning, you are coming out of a weird dream, lying in bed coalescing into wakefulness, and you realize you want to float in water. When you contemplate this unusual notion at times during the week, you feel a deep stirring within you, and it feels as if something from long, long ago is coming through.

There's a lake not far away. You visit their website and discover you can float there! Online you find an appealing float that's affordable. You buy it and after it's delivered one afternoon you stop at a service station, inflate it, and stuff it into the back of your car. You park at the lake and carry it to the shore. There are just a few people out quietly kayaking, and a couple pedal boating. The day is sunny, warm, expansive.

The floating is marvelous. You practically have the lake to yourself, and in the fullness of the late summer ease you let go. You soak in the rays of the sun and your thoughts recede … You lose track of time.

A fresh breeze stirs you and you look at the oaks and pines beyond the shore, standing their ground. There's so much suffering in the world. You want to be as humane as possible. Weeks later when the gracious Indian summer's warmth has waned, one day when you get the mail, rather than throw away an envelope of coupons, you open it. There's one from your car wash, which you save and near the bottom there's a coupon for a float center. Years ago, you'd read about floating in an isolation tank in inches of water saturated with Epsom salt. You make an appointment.

A friendly staff member explains what you need to do.

After showering, you insert earplugs, climb into the pod, and close the hinged door. The saline water matches your skin temperature. The sheer blackness seems endless. You rest your right hand on your tummy and your left over your heart and migrate effortlessly around the large tank. The silence is all-embracing. You can feel your heart beating. It's like being in a womb. You're sure this is far calmer than when you hung upside down for nine months. Thoughts of your mother surface and you imagine them slipping through your head, the salts dissolving them. You're being rewombed.

Remembering the lake, this is so different from the radiant rays streaming into you. You understand that the belief that babies are innocent blinded you. From where and when did that come? Sometime in the scheme of your life, you promised yourself unwittingly that people come into this world with a blank slate. Never questioned, it was a default core belief. Now, that promise has dissolved. You don't know what the sweet baby and her dear mother each did to sow and now reap these days of their lives. You don't know what's arriving in your life, and it's scary and adventurous to not know what's coming and from what action you're reaping today, the next day, and the years to come. You can only do your best, accepting the so-called reality of this life that is only the melting edge of one iceberg among infinite icebergs drifting in an unfathomable sea.

Sometime later, you're aware. Did you drift off to sleep? A soft music comes on. It's time to emerge. Showering off the salt solution, you feel content. From now on, you plan to be more aware to not take anything for granted. You will question things, try to get to the source, accept what's now, feeling and knowing there's much more to life than what's seemingly apparent.

5 The Camouflage of Propinquity

Have you ever been duped? Is it possible that you have been duped and not discovered it?

Do you like, or feel a need, to know what is so? We are living in a world of camouflage. Each of us and everything is disguised. In the way we interact with people and particularly when we attempt to notice, all we see is differentiation. Differences in appearance, behavior, individual circumstance, opinions, actions.

These misperceptions give rise to manifold judgments. With limited perception, we helplessly indulge our calculations—immediate or studied of enemy or friend, how the person or thing can help or hinder us, whether the belief or action is right or wrong. Always judging, always calculating, we are lost in the camouflage and do not see what is so.

The camouflage is the coverings we inhabit. Our bodies and our personhood—all the differentiations we accrue as we go through life. What is being camouflaged? Our soul. Our only true identity. The one existence that is us, for always.

Typically, when people think of camouflage, they picture

soldiers who wear camouflage uniforms and who may color their faces to blend in with the surroundings. They are at war. Animals, birds, fish, and insects practice different methods of camouflage. Chameleons and octopuses, for instance, are adept at changing their skin colors and patterns.

Many people relate to their physical form as a main or definitive source of their identity. They adorn their body with particular clothing, jewelry, makeup, and/or tattoos to change and be something (they are normally not). The payoffs they hope for are manifold—for instance, to look more appealing or to be identified and accepted as one of a group. The troubles and pains some go through, the surgical procedures, to be that different someone who gets to be happy—at least for a short time until they feel deflated and must improve the camouflage. Perhaps for these people, it is a matter of life or death. Imagined or not.

It works better when others buy into the appearance they present. Most important, if they think that now they are being accepted, liked, acclaimed, it delivers self-satisfaction, for as long as it lasts. These camouflage wearers are acting in the service of their mind. But the reality they are buying into, regardless of how well the camouflage does its trick, is bound by the five physical senses along with the mind's perceptions and judgments.

The actual camouflage going on is in the mind. The misperception is seeing and accepting a universe of differentiation. But everything is hiding the one true, abiding reality—God.

The harm and limitation of believing in and accepting the camouflage of our individual differentiation is profound. This fosters the belief of otherness, which acts as growth hormone for the ego. We cannot see through the concealment. Thus, with our oblivious mind and rampant ego, we act unknowingly, causing all kinds of harm. For instance: pursuing our desires at the expense of not fulfilling our duties to family and work. Failing to act kindly and lovingly, thus depriving us and others of whatever love can be exchanged. Killing other living beings and eating those we pay others to kill. Racking up bad karmic debts that will deliver future suffering in our lives and separating us further from God.

The boon of understanding the camouflage and its mastery over us is that we begin to understand and appreciate our shared propinquity. That is, we come from and are of the same Source. Every living thing shares kinship. We are all siblings.

Regardless of evolution of consciousness, every living being shares the spark of soul, that emanation of God that is formless, pure love, and immortal. Everything else is a projection. Why God manifests infinitely diverse progeny we may begin to understand as we meditate and ascend to higher levels of being beyond mind. But the perfect immediate perception of the why of creation can only be truly known when we merge again with the Supreme Being.

In the meantime, we can endeavor to act with the awareness that we are one. Treat every person and every living creature as your beloved sibling. Appreciate that you do not know what burden they are carrying, nor to what extent they are at the mercy of their lower negative mind. True Saints see the Lord in everyone. How would this world transform if we acted as if we enjoyed this awareness and experience?

Imagine the most loving and caring father/mother who asks you and tasks you to believe in our shared propinquity and to think and act accordingly. With this orientation, accepting the at-times harsh and obscure reality in which you find yourself cast, you can find shelter and contentment in the reality of what is so now in your awareness and in the knowledge that you are awakening further.

6   The Vicissitudes of Life

The vicissitudes of life keep rolling in, roiling your equipoise and contentment. Whether it's an unexpected financial setback, the onset of the flu, a visit from a relative with whom you have uncomfortable unfinished business, or missing an important appointment because of traffic, unexpected stuff happens. It is savvy to "expect the unexpected," while keeping a positive detachment about it. To practice being in the now, to live as your most aware self, raises you into greater equilibrium. Responding with the readiness and responsiveness of equilibrium, you are better empowered to deal with any situation that enters your life.

Until you are the master of your mind and its desires, attractions, and expectations, it is easy to be disturbed, at the mercy of your emotions, when the vicissitudes of life engulf you. Where is your peace of mind, your contentment, your ability to detach, gain perspective, and deal with the change with a degree of knowing and mastery that will be in your best interests and induce contentment?

One helpful strategy you can adopt is to accept or pretend that your life is the playing of a script—a scripted so-called reality show. This will engender detachment and mental states that promote actions and nonaction that serve you, rather than disturb you. Instead of playing the situation as craftily as you can—giving your ego free rein—you may wonder if there is a better way that will still handle the situation well but allow you to discover how it may further your spiritual growth.

The vicissitudes of life are your just deserts, the fruit from the seeds that your past actions have sown, but also opportunities to evolve further into your nobler spiritual self. That is the person well worth becoming. Each action, reaction, and thought matters. Negative reactions beget negative ramifications. Cultivate detachment, compassion, and forgiveness for those people who deliver unwelcome speech and action. They are simply playing out their script. Life in this world is not tailored to deliver your every wanted scene and outcome.

If you were a queen or king of an idyllic country with everyone at your command, every happiness would still fade, every day would bring more problems, unforeseen issues you'd like to banish from your queendom.

What is the best you can hope for? What is the path you can seek that will best deal with this ever-changing life?

A daily spiritual practice to which you have committed yourself. That is, a practice you have first thoroughly researched, one you feel will satisfy you, and one with which you are genuinely comfortable. Additionally, when you commit yourself, it is with an independent spirit, not biased by others. Such a path can enable you to rise above and deal successfully with the vicissitudes of life. In turn, this will allow you greater focus on your spiritual life, which can blossom with true inner contentment.

7   The Chimera of Arrival

"... there is no there there."

Gertrude Stein wrote this in *Everybody's Autobiography*. In that famous quote, she stated a universal existential truth. She was writing about returning to the farm in Oakland where she grew up, discovering that "the big house and the big garden and the eucalyptus trees" no longer existed.

When you successfully complete a word game or puzzle, you likely experience a frisson of pleasure. A moment later it is gone. When you take a walk and you're back in your chair, trying to recapture your experience of the walk, where you were is conjured up with the aura of nonexistence. Was it, is it there? You take a long-anticipated trip—say, to the Piazza San Marco in Venice or to Waikiki Beach and Diamond Head on Oahu—and upon arrival you're captivated by the beguiling vision—the place is better than you imagined. But when you return the next day or later it is different. The thrill is not there. You try to conjure up that heightened state, but only a patina of the experience rises in your imagination.

A relative you were fond of—a cousin, a great aunt—comes

to town after years of waiting and weeks of anticipation. They arrive; you visit; you are finally with them. Their visit ends. You view pictures, videos of your time together, but the flat simulacrum does not bring back the good feelings, the reunion, despite how vividly you try to summon it. Their long-anticipated arrival was a chimera.

A chimera is an illusion, a fabrication of the mind. When you do something and seemingly experience the realness of it and then it's over, it's as if it never happened. If you try to relive it, the kaleidoscope of your imagination at best may turn and tease you with evanescent mirages.

Why are gorgeous sunsets so poignant? They arrive unexpectedly, you revel in your moments of witness, and then their beauty fades to darkness. Existence in the physical is a cavalcade of anticipations. When the wished-for experiences arrive in your awareness and you think you are there, in reality, there is no there there.

We are assigned to existing through time with maya beckoning us constantly. We automatically allow ourselves to become attached to the conglomeration of shadow shows. While watching, our limited number of breaths are consumed, and as we arrive at show after show, the limited time we have left seeps away.

Lost are the grace and the intentions to begin to realize your true self. The evolution and arrival of your real self is the only journey that is not a chimera. But you are beset with beguilements at every turn, with each flaming image. This is where intention and commitment are talismans you can summon and empower if you wish to realize your true self, freed of enchantments. That self is an ever-fulfilling state of awareness. Not subject to decay or dissolution, that awakened self ultimately arrives at and returns to its true Home.

8   The Flowering of the Unforgotten

We go about our lives oblivious of the unforgotten. Within us is the most precious, dear, loving part of us. If you look for it, even with the most advanced scientific instruments, you will not find it. But it is there, pervading our entire body. In the onrush and exigencies and sought-after pleasures of everyday life, it is forgotten.

Most of us go to our graves and crematories never having nurtured its inherent glory, never having realized its vast potential for spiritual splendor. That is the fundamental tragedy of human life. Yet the forgotten remains unforgotten by God.

The unforgotten is our soul. That which gives us life and is our connection to God and our potential for God-realization. Because it remains consciously, lovingly unforgotten by God, it is never too late to induce its flowering.

The flowering of the unforgotten can start (or continue) in a multitude of ways, each in accord with the comfort of the individual. For instance, feeling that there is something within you of wondrous beauty that words cannot describe.

Wanting to know the truth about life and death and existence and seeking that truth. Thinking that there must be more to life as we know it and sensing that you can find the way to achieve immortal beatitude. Praying to God for that Infinity of love to become known to you.

Seeking truth. Praying to God. Remembering God in your everyday moments. Having faith that God's presence can be felt by you. Embracing the conviction that you are on a spiritual path, and although much is unknown to you presently, everything can be revealed and known as you continue to evolve and blossom. Acknowledging that at each juncture on your path you can receive the guidance you need.

This may mean seeking and finding a guide. A living guide, who, ideally with your research and best intuition, you come to believe this Guide has realized God. This one, as exalted a human as ever you can imagine, embodies the full flowering of the Ultimate and can show you the true way within.

9   The Beginning of Within

The beginning of within is when you close your eyes. Now the outer world, with all its disturbances, can begin to fade away. It is you and your mind and much, much more. When you focus and collect your attention in meditation at the eye center, between and behind your eyes, you are on the threshold of a new life of superconsciousness.

For eons, your awareness has flowed out through the apertures of the body—your eyes, ears, nostrils, mouth, genitals, and rectum. You have remained incognizant of your inner portal to the mental and spiritual realms. Your eye center is an aperture in your subtle energy body that is located slightly above and behind the physical eyes. By concentrating your attention by means of repetition of a spiritually charged mantra at the eye center, your consciousness can begin to rise, collect, and withdraw through that inner portal and experience the celestial sound and light within.

Your eye center is the seat of the mind and soul. It is the gateway to the "third eye" or "single eye," through which you can gain the subtler, rarefied, *realer* realms of existence. This is the great unknown of most belief systems because they no longer have a *living* Guide who is conversant with and master of the way within and who can initiate seekers into the practice of this meditation of repetition, concentration, and withdrawal.

If you lived in a hovel, would you trade it for a house where you could best be happy? Brought there by your benefactor, you would be wonderstruck everywhere your eye alighted, never imagining that such beauty existed—the art, the design, and décor in accord with you, the gardens in full bloom. You might ask, "What would it cost?" Not a penny: only each day tithing your time to sit and direct your attention from the distractions and entertainments in which you normally engage to being still and focusing within.

Parrots, elephants, dolphins, border collies, and orangutans do not have this opportunity. They lack a third eye. We have that inner aperture, but our mind and soul currents permeate every pore of our body. Only humans can practice this concentrated meditation to collect and withdraw their mind and soul currents and pierce the aperture to ascend to the higher realms of existence and experience ever-increasing bliss.

The realms of existence comprise varying admixtures of three parts: matter, mind, and spirit. Within you are five vast realms or planes, which each contain a seemingly infinitude of worlds.

Our physical plane has the greatest amount of matter of the five planes. As you withdraw your consciousness from the physical world and ascend within, the next higher plane is the astral, called various names by realized Mystics of diverse cultures.

The astral plane has heavens and hells, sub-regions and other regions. The sheer mind-blowing beauty has stopped meditators on their inward journey, believing they had gained the final heaven. They lacked a fully realized Guide who could take them to the far more glorious realms beyond.

Above the astral is the causal plane, also called the mental plane. Here is the least admixture of physical matter. To realize and traverse these planes of consciousness you need a living Guide who has attained the first purely spiritual region that is everlasting.

At the top of the causal is your storehouse of karmas, your vast reserve of debts—good, bad, and seemingly indifferent—accumulated during your myriad lifetimes. Through meditation, concentrated meditation, and more and more concentrated meditation along with the grace of forgiveness, your karmas are eliminated.

Once your slate is pristine, you can pass through what Saints have also called the Tenth Gate to the first of the purely spiritual regions. Until now, your karmas have ruled you. Now your soul has been liberated and attains the realization of being Self, one pure radiance of the Oversoul. You are on your way Home, having transcended the tribulations and dislocations of the lower worlds, realizing finer and finer states of perception, real contentment, pure bliss.

10 The Agency of Authentic Articulation

"In the beginning was the Word, and the Word was with God, and the Word was God."

This is the first verse of the Gospel of John of the King James, Douay–Rheims, and many other versions of the Bible. Its authorship is contested, but most biblical scholars agree that the Apostle John did not author it. Jesus of Nazareth did not author this; nor is there any evidence that these words were taken directly from Jesus, written down, or even exactly remembered and passed along until they were rendered in written form.

Still, this is one of the very most potent lines of belief in Christian faiths, as well as for many who do not identify as Christians. For over two millennia, this verse has exerted sublime agency to inspire longing and engender awe and create wonder at the majesty and mystery of God and existence.

If we do not know for certain whether this is an authentic saying of Jesus of Nazareth, why does its potent agency continue? What is the Word? Is it real? If yes, what is its nature? Its creative power?—if in fact the Word has the power to create. Is it part of the trinity of the Father, the Son, and the Holy Ghost? Is the Word the Holy Ghost?

Is there but one Son for all time? For the billions of humans who have come and gone and for those still alive who are not Christians, are they out of luck? Will they ever be able to meet a Son or Daughter in the flesh?

If God is all-merciful, the Supreme Being is beyond duality and judgment and condemnation. If God is all-loving, the loving Will would facilitate the return of those souls to their original state to be with that One as one for eternity. If God is omnipotent, can Sons and Daughters of God appear in human form when there are those who are ready to return?

It makes sense that the true nature and meaning of the Word can only be shared and explained by a Son or Daughter of God who is living among us, or who has left an authentic articulation of the Word's mystical meaning.

Saints, Mystics, Adepts, Masters, Satgurus, Guides, and Sages across the ages have provided this very spiritual succor for their disciples and followers. They may have lived decades or centuries apart in different parts of the world without knowledge of each other; yet they spoke and wrote about the same mystical path to realize and return to the Godhead. It is a simple matter to research these great realized Teachers to discover they spoke and wrote about the one and same truth and only differed in the names they conferred on the nameless Word to suit their time and culture. Word, Holy Ghost, Logos, Name, Nam, Shabd, Music of the Spheres, Sound Current, Audible Life Stream are all the same.

The Word is the creative emanation of God that is

resounding within each of us. The Word may begin to be experienced within as enthralling sounds and flashes of light when, during meditation, we concentrate the repetition of our mantra sufficiently to collect and withdraw our mind and soul currents and begin to ascend within. It is a gradual process. As we progress within, the Sound Current is experienced as a rapturous unstruck melody and brilliant light. This is perceived through our soul's senses of hearing and seeing. As we realize higher and subtler planes of consciousness imbued with purer spirit, the melody becomes more transporting, the light more brilliant. Descriptions can only hint at what is beyond the physical, which is truer, realer, more abiding than what we have here in this world of darkness and shadow and misdirected questing.

If the Word is within us and, at times without even meditating, echoes can be heard, then having some sense of its divine majesty we can be as cognizant as we can that we are each progeny of God who can realize our inherent ability to speak and write as our higher self, to act with loving kindness, to respect all living creatures because with us they share the indwelling Word. We can sense that we are God in swaddling—that is, we are wrapped in coverings that allow us to live and function on the planes of existence until we realize our true Self and each layer of the swaddling has been released on the journey Home.

Now, even in the physical, we possess unlimited potential to become an authentic *realized* articulation of God. This is our spiritual potential. In our daily lives, we can endeavor to express ourselves with this in mind. Will we issue our expressions from our lower or higher mind?

Be cognizant of the words you express. Words strung together can be missiles, clarifications of purpose, helpful guidance, falsehoods for ill-gotten gains, sweet offerings, self-defeating booby traps, kind encouragements, empowering statements of intention. Words chosen and placed just right articulate our intention, meaning, and humble wishes. Be clear, concise, compelling when you communicate, aware that you are progeny of God. You can be a vital force of the creator of your contentment.

Yes, we are works in progress, *and* we are alive now on the ultimate adventure of becoming. With each thought and action, we either go away from God or toward God.

You can catch your inspiration to articulate your authentic truth. This can serve as an affirmation that will give direction and agency throughout your days. Coin an affirmation that resonates and resounds within you. In the following affirmation this Soul is your true divine Self. How does this feel when you repeat it? Does it open a door?

In the beginning was this Soul, and this Soul was with God, and this Soul is now God forevermore.

11 The Capaciousness of Life

"Thou art God; awake and realize thy glorious destiny."

You may scoff at, wonder about, repudiate, or puzzle over this quote reputed to be from a Saint long ago. This truth-speaking Saint is offering the discovery of your potential. This statement may have kindled a quickening within, a wonderful thrill when you try to imagine the sublime reality.

In the past, you may have prayed to God, wondered about God, bargained with God, rejected God, harshly judged those who naively spoke the word "God." You may have done your best to hew closely to the word of Scripture and/or the teachings of your religious/spiritual identity. That is all fine. But if God is the all-loving force of existence, and if humans have the capacity to seek that Supreme Force, has God simply cast us indiscriminately into this life to suffer *as we each do*, and, to suffer that separation? Is there no hope for redemption?

I don't mean namby-pamby redemption. I mean *real* redemption. "Thou art God; awake and realize thy glorious destiny." If that is true, that's Redemption with a capital "R." True redemption is progressing on your path of spiritualization and ultimately becoming God.

Letting go of the emotionally fraught baggage of the word "sin," let's look at it dispassionately. Redemption or liberation is deliverance from sin. Sin is simply to go away from God. With each act, speech, or thought, we can either move away from God or toward God. To become God, we must be cleansed of sin. We are born with the possibility to begin or continue that process of transformation.

Our limited minds cannot begin to imagine the unfathomable infinite macrocosm of God. The Supreme Being is beyond mind, yet omnipresent in every living and inanimate thing. But if we have been granted the possibility of Redemption, how is it supposed to happen?

Humans have been created with the capaciousness of life within us. That capaciousness of life is accessible by us. We don't need to travel to some distant galaxy or find an alchemical elixir that once drunk will grant us eternal life in these bodies. (Just read some vampire novels to find out how much fun that is.)

No, the true elixir is the divine Sound and Light Current that is coursing within us. God has placed the entrée to the macrocosm within the microcosm of human beings. That's why Saints have said that humans were created in the image of God—our soul is of the same essence of God and, as humans, we possess the inherent ability to realize that consciousness.

By collecting your mind and soul current at the eye center, going within, and realizing higher and higher states of consciousness, you see and hear higher realms of the macrocosm that beggar description because they consist of progressively less matter and more pure luminous, living spirit. That life is more vivid and true and joyous. Within each of us is a capaciousness of life that dwarfs and contains all of the physical universe.

Each of us is not limited to what we are going through now and for the rest of our lives. Anything, everything is possible. Your life to come can far exceed your best imaginings. Of course, you don't know what karmas will form your destinies in future lives. Listen, dear friend, have faith that seeking the capaciousness of life can manifest your best self with the aliveness and love and ease that is available to you.

12 The Misperception of Wakefulness

Have you ever been embroiled in a dream where you struggle to get something right or done, or to get out of a troubling situation? It is all urgently necessary and real. Then you wake up and it dawns on you that you were dreaming. The last images of the dream may ghost through your awareness, but soon absent away as you get on with your day.

Similarly, we are embroiled in our daily lives, often with problems or "issues" if we are cultivating a detached mindset. Work, people, finances, health—it goes on and on day after day: the struggle to forge a good life on Earth. No wonder many of us flock to entertainments that consume our attention, seeking surcease from our troubles.

The delicious elixir of forgetfulness. The game, the show will end and, hopefully, we can segue to bed and sleep with that forgetfulness, enjoying replays of what we've just seen. Ah, sleep. Maybe a lovely dream. Then another day of our customized wakefulness. But how awake are we? How helpful was our escape into forgetfulness? The misconception we lug around day in and day out is that we are awake.

Before we came out of the womb, we were more awake. A few of us retained degrees of access to that greater wakefulness. When the caul of forgetting hardened around our baby heads, we became imprisoned in this lesser reality. We succumbed to the misconception that our daily life, as we were marshaled through it, was our true waking state.

We undertake our daily necessities and pleasures falsely believing that we are awake, but we are not. The acceptance that after hours of sleep being "awake" is our normal state prevents us from finding and following the means by which we can realize successively more wondrous magnitudes of awakening.

When we are pulled out of the physical and pass over to a different stage of consciousness, we will likely remember: Ah! This is how it is. What glory!

That is hardly the beginning. When we dream, the dream state we enter is a lower level of consciousness. How do we know that? We wake up and realize that what was commanding our attention was not real. It was just a dream.

Wakefulness is relative. It depends on the purity of and focus of your attention. Just as our attention descends to the throat chakra or center when we dream, when we enter the eye center with the full focus of our attention, that is the initial awakening of the inner expansion of consciousness. Each higher stage or center realized is a greater state of wakefulness but also reality.

When you pass over, you will ascend to that level of wakefulness, depending on where you were before you took birth and what you achieved this lifetime. To what extent did you realize love and become Love? To what extent were you immersed in the Word, the God Current, the Logos, also known as the Audible Life Stream, the purifier of the mind and Source of your soul?

Who seeks a realized One who can initiate them into this timeless practice of meditation? The beguiling turbulence of this everyday dream keeps us hooked on the false reality. The conceit of the film *The Matrix* is that humans are connected to a simulated reality, the matrix, which intelligent machines have created to distract humans while their bodies are used as an energy source.

Do you wish to remain hooked into your waking dream for the remainder of your life? Sure, you can seek mind-blowing wows, greater comfort, worldly achievement. Here is a key: you can enjoy your limited time here, wherever or however your better passions pull you, and you can also awaken further. The more awake you are, the greater freedom you experience from worry, dissatisfaction, dissonance, emptiness.

Being human means this is your opportunity to dissolve the misconceptions that have barred you from gaining release from this prison house and to grasp your opportunity to begin to wake up and ultimately realize that state in which you are always fully awake. At this level of wakefulness, you enjoy pure perception, an exalted existence.

To gain a truer and better understanding of wakefulness, research the writings and talks of those who have mastered the attainment of higher consciousness and dissolved all misconceptions. For the highest, fully realized Masters exist in and express complete wakefulness. They are physical manifestations of the God Current. They automatically know whatever there is to be known. They are beyond time. They suffer no dream or sleep. They are one with the One. But they can only lead us to them while they live among us in the flesh.

To truly accept and appreciate the ascending heavens of wakefulness you must experience them. Those Masters, Guides, Teachers—whatever you call them—would encourage you to embark on this journey of research, discovery, and experience. Don't take anyone else's word for it. Honor your body as your own mystical laboratory. You will learn and come to know that the refinement of the mind along with the dispelling of misconceptions is a long process that evolves naturally by being a good human being at every opportunity and, critically, by being initiated into the daily practice of meditating on the inner Audible God Current.

Easy to forget this in your mind's onrush of thoughts. Diverted by the mind's occupations and preoccupations, people remain oblivious of their potential of wakefulness. They blindly accept that when they are eating, going somewhere, talking a torrent, they are awake. Wherever you go, whatever you do, remember: this is a misconception. It is remaining imprisoned in a lower consciousness, a much lower level of wakefulness.

For most of us, what impedes our contentment is that we are plugged into the misbelief that we think we are awake in our daily lives. "I talk, I think; therefore, I am awake." That is not true. This is your charge, your platinum opportunity pass to begin to wake up. Realize that you possess latent powers of awakening and attend to your soul's longing to ride the God Stream, gain release from the mind, and merge with the infinite ocean of awakened Life.

13 Developing Discerning Detachment

Stuff happens and we don't know why. We react—we get upset; absorbed, thinking about it; attached, wanting it different; engrossed with what could happen next. We are taken away from our true selves, at the mercy of what is happening outside of us. During these periods of helpless attached attention, how aware are we of our immutable connection to Spirit? Where is our peace of mind? Our inner contentment?

Stuff has been happening to and around people since they walked on Earth. And it's made them scared, exultant, angry, sad, resigned. They've asked: Why me? Why my daughter? My tribe? Yet these acts and happenings are an expression of perfection, however imperfect and wrong we may think they are. Everything is happening according to the highest Will. A critical element of the Will is the metaphysical laws that operate in our physical realm.

One of the fundamental laws of this world is the law of action and reaction. You reap what you sow. You may have a determined dislike of the word "karma." Listen, dear friend, you can't see it, you may not yet know it, but you are bound by it. We are puppets, really, moved by the invisible strings of our karmas—the results of our actions and reactions in our past lives.

Where we have limited free will is in our reactions. No matter how powerful and ingrained are the patterns of our mind, we can make an effort to respond in ways that truly serve us. This is why developing discerning detachment can make the difference between a happy, contented, fruitful life and a life fraught with disagreeableness and disunity from grace.

Stuff happens and everything passes. It is all the karma we have created—sweet and bitter seeds we've sown that have sprouted this life and now we are reaping the fruit of our past actions. Or perhaps sowing new seeds that will lie dormant in our karmic account for untold lives to come. Still, we cling to everything that is foreign and passes: friends, family, work, our dwelling, our love and/or hate objects, our temporary container—that is, our physical body. In truth, none of this is ours. We don't take it with us when we transition to our next assignment.

Being attached to much (and, for many of us, ferociously attached) sows dissatisfaction, disturbance, discontentment. This is not to advocate coldness, a killing of care and human empathy. We would benefit ourselves and others by developing a detached but genuine compassion, for we are all suffering in ways known and unknown. When something happens that is not to our liking, or seems to be what we want, we disserve ourselves by attaching unknowingly to it and investing our energy in the passing show.

Our overriding distresses and delights are steel strings of attachment. Wanting, insisting on a different situation, or craving, expecting something to *stay* keeps us from a glorious inner life. A solid grasp of spiritual teachings that forms the basis of your spiritual foundation is essential to evolving from a life at the mercy of your mind, reacting helplessly to everything around you, to a life of discerning detachment reaping inner riches. Spiritual experiences are real, available, and waiting for you.

Detachment is a release from the programs of your mind—the thought bots that keep popping up, triggering emotions that rob you of your freedom to be joyous. Detachment is an open door through which you can create your spiritual foundation. Aways remember, we are sojourners in this world, bound up in our fates, but not necessarily our reactions. We can choose not to react to any negativity, any affront to our beliefs and sensibilities. We can learn to live on a higher plane above the fray.

You can't force detachment. The mind's thoughts and emotions keep coming back. Yet, with our limited free will, you can mentally step back from the passing show and exercise your observer muscle. You can then find that space of freedom to choose and direct your response, or no response, in a way that serves you as well as others. It is accepting that people act the way they do even if they wish they could act differently. But they follow the dictates of their mind and, if the lower mind is predominant, which it is for most people a majority of the time, they can't help themselves. Hence: awareness, detachment, compassion. Discover how to work with your mind. Serve yourself by feeling confident that you can advance in spiritual enlightenment. Explore the next phase that path may take.

You may realize that true detachment comes from that which is more powerful than the mind. That which awakens the finer spiritual senses and direct perception. True detachment comes from that which automatically attaches the mind to something far higher and more beautiful than the busy, distraught traffic of our thoughts. Detachment must be cleansing, utterly beautiful, mystically uplifting, and rapturously reminding us of who we truly are.

That is soul reawakening in the Sound Current. An emanation of the indwelling, unifying field of Spirit. The better you realize that connection, that truth, the greater your immersion in the peaceful, blissful flow of spirit. And the stronger your attachment to spirit, the closer you are to realizing yourself, your true self.

14 The Heroism of Subjugation

Action!

You are the hero of your life. While this movie of your life proceeds, you will play many roles: playmate, sibling, coworker, spouse. How well you act in all the scenes you are called to appear in will very much determine the experience of your mind, the refinement of your character, the quality of your life, and your fundamental contentment.

People with whom you interact, and God, will witness your outer behavior. Only you will be cognizant to whatever degree you are of what is going on inside your head. God will know all. To play well with good intention, honesty, positivity, and grace—if that is what you wish, if that is what you are called and inspired to do—you will need to be aware of what is going on inside that beautiful head of yours.

What thoughts are percolating? What past put-downs and meannesses are replaying in your mind as you go about your day? Are you fully present and meeting each moment with positive engagement?

Until we have mastered the mind, we are *subject* to it. We are captives, besieged when we least expect it, for instance, remembering when past friends, long-exited from our life, were mean to us. At that time, they only had that awareness and the expressed words and actions that pierced your heart. Why do they continue to hurt you? That festering wound has been rubbed over, played over again and again. Perhaps if at some point you had mustered the wherewithal to communicate wisely and kindly the experience of your hurt, healing would have occurred, and now that mental version would no longer invade your awareness villainously.

Is the person or company or institution that hurt you the villain? Perhaps might it be your negative thoughts? That scene is past, but the negative tendencies of your mind continue to reenact it. You could be enjoying wonderful thoughts and feelings, elevating your experience of life in the now; yet negative thoughts appear in scene after scene agitating your calm of contentment. They deprive you of peace and dynamic equilibrium, which are in your power to enjoy and make the most of out of your remaining life.

It takes a certain awareness to be conscious of your thoughts and images throughout the day. It takes courage and commitment to subjugate the down-pulling thoughts in the way you presently know best. It is much easier to go through the motions of your activities unconsciously, or disappear into media. But this is a battle for your very life. This is your call to be and act as the hero of your life and enjoin your nobler self to defeat your negative mind and emerge victorious. Be assured, however, that God's grace will be with you regardless of your awareness.

Rather than allowing the negativity of your lower mind

to bamboozle you whenever and however it will, you have the ability and power to muster your innate heroism. Because God is the fount of goodness, of positivity and is *within* you, you possess the power to draw on the positivity to nullify and rise above negativity. Why is there such rampant unbridled strife in the world? We allow our ego's negative passions to rule us.

Heroism is summoning the earnestness to sacrifice the entrenched, ignoble small self. That is, the presently dominant self that allows its endless desires to demand fulfillment. And you are never being truly fulfilled. Seeking the satisfaction of your mind's every wish keeps the best you at bay, while your lower mind acts out with such overwhelming constancy that you identify with it. Rather than heedlessly allowing your mind to spout its negativity as is its will and wont, observe it and gain knowledge of how it undermines your contentment. When you sense that you are at a fulcrum point and a knowingness bathes your mind and something shifts, you can resolve that subjugating your lower mind's negativity is the worthy ongoing project for realizing yourself further.

If you are reading or listening to this book then you have already made an investment in realizing your best self. That self is a reflection of the goodness of God. But how do you go about subjugating the negative bots of your mind? Regardless of what you may be doing, of the higher focus you may be practicing, the thought bots keep popping up in your awareness and you have probably been identifying with them all along, indulging them at the expense of your contentment.

A truth is that your higher self, your best self, does not

alone have the power to subjugate your rogue mind and ego. Unless you are a realized Master who has mastered the mind, your lower mind has been directing you ever since you grimaced with your first pout to get what you want, ever since you threw your first tantrum to get the scene to play to your selfish needs. Drama queen that you have been, let's look further at ways to subjugate your lower mind.

Why not adopt the practice of offering each of your actions to God? Being and acting with God present however it feels best and/or visualized is a potent way to elevate yourself and transcend your lower mind. You can evoke and/or envision the Presence. You can practice this before a meal when you offer gratitude, when you are walking somewhere, or when you are taking time out to gaze at whatever is before you. Before long, as you integrate this practice into certain times of your day, it will become a habit you welcome and gradually a way of empowering your higher mind and keeping the down-pulling mind at bay.

Remember that love conquers all? Any way that feels good, you can summon the omnipresent, all-abiding love of your soul to shine through and enliven your nobler self. Your soul, which is, in reality, an immortal particle of God, is the self you can ultimately realize. This call to commitment along with the humble surrender to God to show you the way can supercharge your journey of becoming.

As to becoming, daily meditation is showing up to transcend the mind and allowing God to consort with you. If your present meditation is one of watching your thoughts and/or breath, when nagging, negative thoughts pop up, you can learn to neutralize them in accord with your practice and allow a positive focus to experience a higher state.

If you wish to vaporize your lower mind and actively focus on the God Stream within, you can seek a realized Master who will initiate you into the practice of the Sound Current. No matter how faint and far away it may seem, this emanation of God of inner Sound and Light is the surest way of subjugating your lower nature and evolving into Love.

To confront the freewheeling mastery of your mind takes courage. Your mind will want to saturate you with ennui and laziness. It will rationalize convincingly on what you deserve and need to do to take you away from your struggling spiritual investment, which is paying dividends—mainly unforeseen at present. You may feel defeated again and again, but pay no mind—you are a hero of your destiny and you can always take up arms to do your best to slay the many-headed beast and go with God. Yes, now you have summoned your heroism and you can encourage yourself to evolve moment by moment, trusting that God's infinite reward comes as Love knows best.

15 Consciousness Continues

Yes, it does.

Don't worry. Be curious.

You are alive now. Why not take advantage of it?

No doubt, the thought of your own death has crossed your mind. Now is your chance to find out as well as you can whether your consciousness will continue after you die. This could give you great solace. To many, even the thought of death is forbidden. It overwhelms with loathing and fear. It is too awful to entertain. It must be overridden. That's one reason people lose themselves in outer entertainments.

Be caring with yourself. You are going to die—*this* lifetime, that is. The specter of your death may be a paramount antagonist to your contentment. It need not be. You can use this coming reality to your advantage. Nothing is wasted. Life goes on. Like a wave, life rushes in, filling a form. Then it rushes out, leaving the physical matter to return to its natural elements.

Levels of consciousness exist. You may not be able to find out this lifetime what your consciousness will be after you die, but your consciousness will continue. Naturally, there is a fear of the unknown. You have died so many, many, many times before. You will get through it and be aware on the other side, according to your evolution.

Regardless of your destiny—this fate you are going through that has been culled from your past actions—this lifetime is your starring performance in your very own prime-time show that airs for an allotted number of hours and breaths. While you are hitting your marks and saying your lines, how will you be in your awareness? Will you be expressing yourself toward higher consciousness or away? Will you entertain every negative impulse that fixes your attention? Will you allow every coarse emotion to outburst? Or, when the impulse is to go negative, will you summon your fullest compassion and discerning cogitation to allay the negativity?

Knowing that almost everyone is an unwitting subject of their mind, which is a sop to the senses, you can live with this awareness, identify negativity for what it is, and even imagine the full flowering of consciousness. Consciousness is a vast spectrum that you cannot begin to know fully until you transcend the mind.. Consciousness extends beyond mind. That means no thought. It is extralingual consciousness, direct perception.

The higher your consciousness, the more *realized* it is to its fullest potential. And the closer you are to being who you truly are: pure exalted consciousness, a state of divine love.

Each day, you can further the journey of realizing who you truly are. You can access and develop your sense of higher knowing moment to moment. If you are so moved, you can seek a path of meditation that fits right with you and practice it. And remember: your mind has been going out and down for an inconceivable accumulation of time. You can reverse the flow. You can summon your will. When this sojourn on Earth ends, what will you take with you?

16 Pellucid Perception

When an immediate perception comes, you may notice it or not. If you notice it, it may register or not in your awareness. If it registers, you may utilize it or not.

At times, we are graced with immediate knowing. Something comes through—you're immediately aware of something—it's an action to take, a needed bit of information, a guidance that is extralingual. Your mind may or may not translate it into language. It often comes so unexpectedly that you are unaware of it. If you are aware of it and it registers in your awareness, this adds to your transformation.

A pellucid perception is a perception that is known, registers, apposite in the now. The immediate knowing lusters your higher mind with truth, thus refining and rising it to a higher level. It lusters your being by spreading the light of truth within your consciousness. A perception that is pellucid lusters your consciousness by bringing forth your soul's inherent luminosity.

To what does a pellucid perception harken? It harkens to the fundamental nature of humans—that we are capable of pure perception. This surpasses thought and language. The experience of and potential for pellucid perception harkens to who we really are—soul. Once we attain self-realization on the inner spiritual journey, our consciousness has transcended mind. We are pure soul. We know by direct perception; the soul is the actual knower.

Our potential is to become one with the Oversoul, the infinite, eternal Source from whence we originated. The glimmers that flash through give us encouraging enhancements of becoming Truth, another name for the nameless One.

17 Forgetfulness

The world is raging in a pandemic of forgetfulness. We have forgotten who we are, from whence we came, and we must suffer what will come. We have forgotten the basics: how to be a good human being, to be kind, virtuous, truthful, and how to be our better self; rather we are an amalgam of impulses, desires, thinking, and acting at the behest of whatever commands our attention one moment to the next.

We remain confidently, indulgently ingenuous that our every action gives rise to a reaction, for the challenge bestowed on humankind is forgetfulness. We have devolved (some unwillingly, most enthusiastically) to the state that we believe we won't reap what we sow. We are divorced from the reality and knowledge of consequence. Yes, death will come, at times a dim or poignant warning that is soon overrun by the onrush of whatever next captures our attention. But all those inflicted hurts and good deeds have consequences. At some point in our assured ongoing journey through existence, we must show up and live through the reaping of our deeds.

The sad state of affairs of humankind is that we are cast back into the world, reborn to too soon forget what we have suffered in past lives. Even the sufferings of this life are for-gotten—the illnesses, betrayals, aborted dreams, squelched hopes, the loss of loved ones—in having to show up for the next thing. This is a general rule of life: to forget from whence we came and who we truly are; to live and create conse-quences and, unbeknownst, live through the consequences of our actions, *and* to miss the opportunity to win a permanent Get Out of Jail Free card and *return* to a glorious existence.

Yes, there is a way out of our constantly beckoning laby-rinth, from which we are removed when it is our time, only to be thrust into the next labyrinth to struggle through yet again. Forgetfulness has antidotes. Mercy and grace are always available.

Some are blessed with involuntary awakenings of expanded higher consciousness. Yet others, such rare ones, are *fully* conscious. They do not need to remember, for they *know*. These are the Saints, Masters, Adepts who live among us as realized humans, who have come to initiate those who are ready to play the transformational game of life. You can search for one, and you can also find and read their writings to reorient your mind and prepare you for the amazing grace when you are found.

Their teachings, their writings, can trigger memories, can resonate with your innermost being to help you advance on your journey of seeking and remembrance. This may strike you as airy-fairy stuff and may not appeal to you. The thoughts issuing from your mind and your senses, beckoned by all this world hopes to offer may easily pull you away, and once again you will grope willingly along the pathways of forgetfulness.

Lost in the forgetfulness, one thing after another will capture your attention and life.

Forgetfulness is incessantly appealing. Surging with desires, you can forget your forgetfulness and surrender just like the others—chasing your drives and desires, steeping yourself in sensation, determined to be oblivious of suffering, grasping at your paper straws of contentment to suck up your welcome drink of oblivion. Enjoy for a time, until your straw dissolves. The underlying truth remains: we are spirit, one of the One, the top of the creation, thus fully self-realizable, able to seek and become again the Truth that is beyond the creation.

But your mind's willfulness can readily overrun any intimation, any remembrance of that eternal connection, and grasp the next thing outside yourself. The world runs on forgetfulness. It's cool, seductive, easy, rote, comforting, and oh, so familiar. The force of the world—everything around you is beseeching you to keep forgetting, to follow your impulses and thoughts wherever they lead you to think, say, and write whatever strikes your fancy regardless of the hurt it may cause you and others. But hurts perpetrated by others against you—that is one thing remembered, oft nursed. When that hurt is relived enough in your thoughts (along with your imagined retorts to the injuring party), it becomes an unresolved groove and mandates that eventually you will get your retribution. You won't know to what it was originally connected—you will be in another body.

Yes, we receive pain and gratification covered with our caul of unknowing. Why and from whence the experiences come is veiled by the passage of lives in the physical. Lives lived yet again with the caul of forgetfulness. Lost in sensation, forgetfulness can feel luxurious, high, grand—even seemingly ennobling for those bravely bearing troubles, disease, and injustices while congratulating themselves on being valiant. Regardless of anyone's expression of ego, the rest of us can let go of judgments and instill compassion for all those caught up in this play of life.

But the better, ultimately rewarding pain is the one that remains buried by the onrush of life. This special pain is one of which you are likely unaware. If you are unaware and will remain so for the remainder of your days, you are immune from experiencing this signaling pain of yearning. The forgetfulness of what lives we've lived, of who we truly are is the all-purpose vaccination of coming into this world. Some babies and young ones can at moments recall elements of their time before and promises they made to remember. But then ...

Is it too late? You can still listen to and nurture the sure, quiet voice within. Your soul is *yearning* to empower your nobler mind to be its ally to help you commence your return Home. That is the God-given path within you that banishes forgetfulness.

18 Unhappiness

For most of my years, I was an unhappy person. This was so despite years of therapies starting when I was eighteen. The unhappiness was for three specific reasons. First, for not being able to live as a full-time writer. Second, for not being able to find and enter into a loving, supportive primary relationship. And third, for the lack of love in my life. Here I was, supposedly on the path of love to reunion with God, LoveSource, but I did not *feel* love or loved. This may have had more than a little to do with having been blessed with an unloving family whose various members committed emotional abuse, physical and verbal abuse, infant abuse, and preschooler rape. This is the therapeutic gift that keeps on giving.

I did feel ardent love and devotion toward my meditation Teacher, but this relationship was troubled, as I felt terribly anguished about being gay. This path's strict moral vow included the injunction that sexual relations were to be confined within the marriage of a man and woman. Homosexuality was considered a crime against nature. Of course, trying at best to be budding saints, people were human. Once gay marriage began to be legalized, I felt that its legality in Spain (where our Teacher had lived) would prompt a sea change in the vow. And yes, not until Spain legalized gay marriage did my path change its guidelines years later. I felt better after forty-four years of often feeling tortured by the agony of being deemed an unnatural human. From the age of twenty-one—way ahead of the times—I wanted to be married to a man and I let myself endure decades of mental torment simply for being gay and for not finding a partner.

Still, I craved love. When the odd friend (or stranger) was simply kind or sweet to me, I treasured that. What kept me going, I suppose, was the blissful love that suffused me when I saw my Guide or after a particularly effortful meditation when, least expected, I felt flooded with grace and love.

But how did I surmount the nagging unhappiness? By continuing to devote myself to my spiritual path. By having my desires ground down. I kept the writing alive by writing fifteen to twenty minutes a day and a little more on Saturday, while plying my demanding tax practice and dealing with my many chronic health challenges. My first two published books—spiritual books—were a surprise in my late forties. When I was twenty, I had started a novel and felt that being a writer was to be my life's calling. But the novel was put aside to complete my senior year at the University of California at Berkeley. The call to write would surface from time to time, but with the necessity of earning a living and my immersion in my spiritual path, I would let it recede in my consciousness. It was not until I was thirty-three, that I resolved to set out on my writer's path.

The two books came out at a most difficult time—my

biological father was fading away and then died. My biological mother became like a wild teenager with freedom for the first time. Further, my violent, very paranoid-schizophrenic brother was acting out. Finally, we landed him in a boarding house.

Then I entered a writing wilderness, trying all kinds of writing: a spiritual reality show mainly to create a platform to sell *more BLISS*, the sequel to *BLISS*, my second published book. Essays. Short stories. It was not until 2013 when I began to recover my past lives that I truly delved into writing again, not knowing, not thinking it would become a book and even be published. But it was. With the publication of *In Search of Lost Lives*, the frustration I felt as a writer dissipated and dissolved. Also, with my ego worn down through years of effort, I was now more available to heed my higher guidance and give myself to the fascination and love of whatever I was writing.

I do not know anyone who put more effort into looking for a partner: personal ads, going out (just hoping to meet someone), group activities, speed dating, even a matchmaker. I never came remotely close. After my major small bowel resection, many partial and total insanely painful bowel obstructions, and subsequent surgery to reduce the massive growth of scar tissue and adhesions, the desire for a partner and sexual interest disappeared. It had been waning before that, but the two surgeries and the years-long struggle to survive—to eat intuitively and so carefully *as much as I could* and *not too much* to not suffer another bowel obstruction freed me of the quest for a primary partner connection. I found myself more and more content being single and free. Enjoying what I enjoyed. Continuing as ever with my meditation. Writing. Reading. Preparing and enjoying my tiny meals.

The updating of the moral code of my meditation path coupled with the falling away of the apparent need to find a partner brought more contentment. My three main reasons for being unhappy were resolved. I was happy in my meditation, regardless of how scattered I seemed to be.

But what is unhappiness? What causes unhappiness? *Desire.* Unfulfilled desires. Fulfilled desires that do not fill you and, if they do for a time, the mind wants more. New or recycled wants consume your awareness. The key for me was to become attached—immersed—to something higher within myself—the true source of love. Spirit. Summoning the presence. Feeling, listening for and to the Sound Current, LoveSource, the real abiding love. Even if I did not feel the heart-bursting, happy-swooning emotions in the ways our culture often portrays love, my effort, steadfastness, and pursuit of my spiritual purpose were the real thing. This is what brings me happiness.

19 Heaven Can't Help Us

Yes, Emma, dear grandniece, there is heaven, for you perhaps, but it can't help you. Not truly help you. What you dream of as heaven is much, much grander—a vast realm of life teeming with endless varieties of gorgeous possibilities of sights and sounds, beings and experiences. If you are rewarded with heaven (seemingly for your good deeds), you will linger there perhaps for a seeming eternity, even with your loved ones from this life who may or may not be who you think they are.

This heaven is so vast—beyond anyone's comprehension—that you cannot imagine the multitudes of worlds and celestial domains existing within this grand heaven, and after this life of yours, if you dedicate yourself to performing good deeds without any expectation of reward, you may very well be rewarded with a stay in your own heaven.

You may rejoice in your own heaven that you will be there forever, but you know what? You think you now have eternal life—and you do—but you have eternal life passing through many lives as different life forms, though they are all you. Perhaps you were a samurai in an earthly life in medieval times in the country called Japan in English. Pretty exciting, yes? You were a noble warrior doing good on orders from your lord. In that life, you lopped off sixty-seven heads, accumulating great honor for your clan and you (and causing excruciating pain to those who lost their heads).

Unbeknownst to you, everything has a price. There's a ruler way, way more powerful than your medieval lord, and he has a perfect system of keeping score. So guess what? Your stay in your perfectly tailored heaven will end. You will leave your so-perceived family and friends to face the result of the suffering you caused by lopping off all those heads. That will not be fun. That will be far from heaven while you go through the equivalent of that suffering during enough lives on Earth or somewhere worse to even the score.

But dear Emma, don't be scared. You've probably been a very good person—at least, you have been a very good girl this lifetime. The truth is, the heaven you've been dreaming about is a teensy element of the first of seven grand heavens. These seven grand heavens or regions are vast realms each vaster than the one before, existing in higher, finer, subtler energies, each one more brilliant with enrapturing celestial melodies of primal sounds and living colors. No words can begin to describe the beauty of these heavens and your most fertile imagination cannot begin to picture the luminous beings that exist in higher and higher states of love as you progress from one heaven to the next.

Even if you find yourself in the second region—a wondrous realm of heavens—there you can get trapped. You are still operating with your mind rather than pure soul. While residing in that second heaven *can* help you experience utterly gorgeous sights, exercise the most extraordinary powers to manifest what you desire, and consort with the exalted beings, you still may have to come back to be born again to face the effects of the good and bad deeds you committed in the past. The only one who can help you is the right Teacher, a Guide, who has liberated herself from her mind while still alive in her body and passed through the second heaven to the third heaven. From there, you can only advance as far as she has.

Imagine you were the lone young person in a spaceship traveling to a far distant galaxy that existed beyond a black hole. But as soon as your ship approached it, its alien frequencies fried the crew's brains. No one could operate the ship— they were dead. But you, dear girl, being younger and more vital, were alive and having already been taught the basics of navigation could theoretically find a way to pass through the black hole but had no idea how to, let alone avoid all the unforeseen dangers.

You see, to pass through the third heaven to the fourth, you have to pass through an impenetrable darkness. Only a realized Guide, who originally passed through the darkness with *her* Guide and came back to her body where she was meditating while she still resided on Earth, can *help you*. If you met such an advanced Guide while both of you were still alive here, she could ultimately take you through each heaven as you became purer and purer love.

Eventually, way beyond the confines of time, she could guide you to realizing the fourth heaven. Such longing you will feel for the fifth Heaven, your true, everlasting Home. You can revel in the ceaseless wonders in the playing fields of God. You can realize the sixth and seventh Heavens and even that is not the Ultimate, for beyond the seventh heaven is the exultant eternal estate of LoveSource.

20 Death by Fallow Imagination

Many are the people who die from fallow imagination. They remain oblivious of the possibility of possibilities and suffer lives less lived. Opportunities left unnoticed. Paths not taken.

There is always a way to resolve any situation. Not only a person's actual death, but a thousand life-deaths en route to their looming departure. Life-deaths are accepted incursions of negativity that keep you from advancing in your best life. By gathering information and using clear thinking, along with your native intuition and imagination, you can navigate your individual spiritual path.

Regardless of our circumstances, many of us lead an impoverished life. Now, we likely cannot begin to imagine what we are truly suffering. We may not even have an inkling of it, nor ever register a fleeting feeling of the inner riches awaiting us, so oppressed are we by the necessities of daily life and our driving, demanding thoughts. We may embrace the drudgeries of life—with resentment or with welcome relief because they keep ominous death at bay—but a *luminous life*, infused with spirit, always awaits us. Though it is available to us, we have relinquished our power and will and allowed our imagination to lie fallow.

We are suffering death by fallow imagination. We all possess the faculty to cultivate a fertile imagination that will bring forth rich growth and life fructification. With this engagement, you can enjoy an invigorated spiritual life. Happiness and contentment can bloom.

You may automatically think: How can I add to my life? What people might I cultivate; what more money can I make; what sensual pleasures can blow my mind? By revving up your imagination in the traffic of the world, you may give precedence to sensual transport and ego balms, but these pleasures and satisfactions readily fade away. Your imagination is chiefly for you to figure out life as best you can and also to win the contentment that comes from awakening further and preparing yourself for the best life beyond this one.

You can exercise your imagination to discover and cultivate your divine connection within—that is, your soul being one of the One. You can imagine and discover how to sow the seeds that will sprout and grow toward the spiritual light within you that is always present, despite the current dominance of your mind. You can use your imagination to learn how to be devoted to your spiritual connection throughout the day. If you feel an inner prompting, you can visualize God in human form with you at breakfast, standing close by when you're on the toilet, near you to sweeten your sleep as you slip away to a blessed slumber.

A person with little to their name, with only the basics of adequately clean air, water, food, shelter, and clothing, can lead the richest life simply by cultivating and attending to their divine Presence within. Similarly, a person with all the material comforts they could hope for but leading a life of isolation or filled with negative people can awaken to a life of true inner riches.

Complacency and passivity are the quagmires that cause life-deaths. Fallow imagination causes the failure to explore. We may be stuck, lost in our day after day, and not know it or, at times, inklings may flit across our awareness. Loyalty to habit can be dangerous. We may be consorting with people who are truly not good for us or wasting life in patterns of consumption that once provided some engagement and balance but still took us away from ourselves. Surcease from the aggravations of life by indulging your lower mind's go-to passions is the customary way to use up your life.

Many of us would do anything to avoid feeling any mental discomfort, let alone collapsing in a hollow of *Weltschmerz* (German: translated literally as "world pain"). But perhaps this is telling you that you are missing out on an opportunity. Rather than losing yourself to whatever else can capture your attention, staying in this trough of unknowing, you can activate your imagination to explore and follow in your mind's eye what this life has to offer you *and* activate your *will* to find out what is best for you.

Why not find a quiet time when you can relax, let go, and imagine yourself as an evolved human with the most beautiful qualities? You possess all the virtues and spiritual strengths within you and the potential to realize them fully. Imagine a perfectly cut EightStar diamond dazzling with colorful fires.

But it has fallen out of its setting and landed on the ground, which after a storm became mud. Trod upon, the diamond became buried and, when the ground dried, encrusted with dirt. One day a gardener was troweling a bed for flowers and discovered the very hard stone. After washing it thoroughly and holding it up to the light, the brilliance of the diamond was recovered.

That is our condition, too. Having taken association with the mind, our brilliance of soul has been buried by the accumulated dross of actions and reactions, desires and attachments.

How can you get to the more brilliant you? Imagine what steps you might take to evolve to your full potential. If you are moved to, note or record what comes to you. Look up questions that arouse your curiosity. What else can you explore? Let questions and ideas flow through your awareness as you go about your day. You may receive prompts that pique your curiosity. Perhaps one is finding and listening to an interview about human potential. Or following a social media group that exudes good, high positivity. Or perhaps your higher knowing might prompt you to find the next book that calls to you.

Life is full of choices. Sometimes it seems like we're facing an overflowing buffet. At other times, though, the options can be a dilemma; none are a sure thing, none feel like a good choice. You may be faced with competing paths or priorities the cons of which seem to outweigh the pros. This may now be the time to gather as much information as you need (if you're not already fully informed). Or it may be a good idea to use your imagination along with your intuition to suss out the right person to talk to, as they may better inform you and, regardless of their opinion, serve to reveal how you truly feel about the options.

You can use your imagination to feel and picture the divergent paths the options represent. Try asking your higher self key questions: Which choice, which option has the best possibility of allowing more peace? Which will allow me to be closer to God? Keep asking, keep seeing in your higher mind's eye, allowing time for the process and for your imagination to grasp the situations so you can resolve the dilemma. You can always pause and do nothing about the options until a knowing blooms within you.

The potential of your awareness is unlimited. As you establish a growing relationship with your higher self, you will be able to tap into the great resources within to explore the options of *any* situation using your innate intuition along with your imagination.

For many, the ultimate dilemma is death. For most of us, death is the unimaginable. And the default is letting yourself get lost in the world, unaware of the commanding prerogatives of the mind, which has forgotten *its* true home. The mind's true home is universal mind, at the top of the mental plane. In this life, with the foreboding unknown bearing over you, you can be taken out any time. If you bother to know what's going on in the world, you're shown this daily. It is prudent to make sound and legal preparations for your health care, pet care, and your assets in the event of incapacitation or death. Aside from this, you may use your imagination to wonder: Will I truly die?

You can use your imagination to explore the questions of death. Listen, dear friend, there is so much to explore!

Human beings who are Saints or Masters, who are from God or who have attained that achievement of consciousness during this lifetime, have been among us throughout history across lands and cultures. In plain language, in parables they have revealed to us that the way out—of death—is in. Use your fertile imagination. Would an all-merciful Supreme Being preclude the way to return to that all-loving forever?

Certainly, the planes of material and mental-material existence function with universal laws. We are subject to them. But a true, ardent heart of devotion wins grace and favor. These fully realized Saints and Masters pass through the gate of death daily—as readily as slipping off an overcoat. Imagine—a human who is with us, at our level *and* God's. And they are among us to show us the way home and guide us within via mystic realization and transport.

Regardless of whether you are ready to return, by spading your imagination you are enriching it. And by encouraging new ways of being, you can enjoy splendid growth. You can learn easier ways of dealing with the issues of life and how to explore and elevate your living so your existence continues expanding ever more consciously.

Just imagine.

21 The Teachable Dweller

You are a teachable dweller. Right now, you are dwelling in the physical living under a shroud of unknowing. But you possess all the knowing within you. What's critical is that you have the innate sense of knowing to *teach yourself* how to live experience after experience in the way that serves you best.

We are here temporarily in the physical because of our actions in our past lives that begat reactions. We are here due to our *reactions* to what we experienced. But we are also here because we are teachable. Our destiny continues to unspool as we unknowingly play our parts pulled—as puppets, really—by the strings of our destiny. Much of our destiny is a struggle, a slog. We get ourselves further karmically hamstrung with heedless mean words, insistent desires, greedy actions, being responsible for death after death of innocent lambs, chickens, and salmon. The killing goes on; you rack up more debts. Each of us goes through our destiny, creating destinies to come, *and* we can use experiences as opportunities to evolve spiritually, or they can bind us to more indebtedness.

It can surely seem ridiculous, unfair, unscientific to write that you have a destiny—unseen and unknown. The truth is you are a puppet being pulled by the strings of your destiny. But this is the play in which we find ourselves. Scene follows scene, act after act until your play is finished. Then your sojourn here is over until you reenter another stage. So many actors—family, schoolmates, coworkers—have long exited your current play, and before long you will find yourself in another state upon death, then another sojourn, in a state of consciousness that depends on your spiritual evolution and just consequences. Quite possibly you will get to review your life and get an idea of how you did and realize what you need to work on next time. But then, there is no assurance that next time you will get a human birth.

When you think, when you go through experiences, each time is a teachable moment. You can either react with your downward-pulling passions of ego, anger, greed, and more, creating negativity and further binding karmas. Or you can consciously respond, marshalling your best resources to be kind and understanding, as detached and humble as you can be. You can refrain from judging others and yourself.

Why not envision yourself, the highest, most loving aspect of your infinite self, as the best, most responsible teacher you can have now. You can do it. You may well come across especially wise persons, seemingly compelling experts, even teachers who help you further your human potential. But they cannot do it for you. They can't change you. You need to inculcate the best of their wisdom that rings true, along with you own intuitive best knowing, and teach yourself.

You will begin to sense better and better when and how to refrain from hurtful remarks. When and how to avoid needless and detrimental confrontations. You will become open to knowing how to serve your fellow sojourners. We are all struggling. But most are struggling to get ahead in the world, to satisfy ever-recurring lusts, to find love in the world.

For now, you are a dweller on Earth, this rough smudge of mud, rock, hurricanes of hard knocks, goodness when it shines through. You are leaving. You will play out your play and, during it, you can develop the awareness to be a teachable dweller, taking note of how you goofed up, remembering to be better next time. You can also resist attention magnets to which your everyday mind is automatically pulled but which do not serve you. Resisting and letting go of things you truly do not need and which dye you in murky shades creates freedom, brings heart-relieving contentment.

Be cognizant that you have a destiny beyond your ken. Puppet strings of gold, iron, copper, or silver—they're all the same. Act as though you have free will. This puppet play of your life continues until the final scene. You can do your best to be in equilibrium and comport yourself and respond with grace, even finding the feeling that you are completing the karma and not adding more to your account. Cultivate the intention and the awareness to be detached from outcomes, during and after each situation. When you allow events or circumstances to trigger your harsh reactions, you extend your contracts for further appearances back in the physical, often with unfortunate, regrettable events. Many a beatific saint endured excruciating torments, yet they responded with aplomb and love.

You can be saintly from time to time, leading *your*

authentic life while maintaining your individual equilibrium. A key element of becoming an adept teachable dweller is knowing how it feels when you are in equilibrium, a state of dynamic balance with a comfortable, quiescent mental state. For this is when you are more apt to be wise and not react negatively, creating new karmic debts. When you find yourself out of sorts, in disequilibrium, you can teach yourself to return to that benevolent state of equilibrium. It may be to watch a light, engaging show after a hard day of work. It may be meditating. Or walking. It's up to you. Take responsibility and discover each time what calls you back to equilibrium.

Learning to teach yourself, to be your best with detachment and to do your best, is a loving act. This transforms your whole experience of being here. In time you will realize you are a much different person than you were ten years ago, even four years ago. It can seem as if you are in a different play. Keep a journey journal if you are so moved. When you read entries of years ago and read those past states of mind, those worries, those different people in your life, it may seem that you are now in another lifetime.

Saints may sometimes say that we do not learn from our mistakes. Most of us don't remember the hurtful acts we committed in past lives, let alone know the consequences of what we suffered. We may be captive to the scripts of our destiny, playing out in physical or mental spaces luxurious or grungy, but we can endeavor to be our best selves in each situation, with the intention to please God, treating ourselves as the most kind, patient, understanding parent would.

Can you finesse your destiny *this* lifetime? That is something to meditate on. You can experience the gratitude of being in a situation, *but this time,* being aware and comporting yourself in a way that best serves you and is kind to others. That brings contentment that yields dividends.

22 Awaken Your Discernment

Each of us is endowed with the power of discernment. It can make the difference between a life lived knowingly and a life lived bumblingly. Your soul is all-knowing. Unless you are truly wholly enlightened, the soul is enshrouded with wrappings and layers of mind that obscure the light within. The auspicious reality is that discernment can be developed and your higher mind empowered so your soul's light can begin to filter through to your awareness.

It can be as simple as asking, "Is this true?" And asking it of your higher consciousness, feeling as well as you can the connection with soul. Rather than reacting or charging into a situation impetuously, unknowingly, it can be well worth your while to pause and discern what is at play and at stake.

If personalities are at play, get a feeling as to how they are being ego driven. You can rise above any negative situation by being neutral, nonjudgmental, nonreactive. Remember: most people are puppets—flailing about and expelling verbiage to the discordant tunes of their mind. And the noise that issues from them can go from mild to cutting without warning.

If you are faced with a decision, a response, discern what

would love do. If you were a realized embodiment of love, awareness, forgiveness, and equanimity, what would you do or communicate? Being this, keep in mind: that you would never want to hurt another's feelings; to what extent, if any, you are being ruled by the down-pulling passions of anger, greed, ego, and more; that you are seeking to adjust toward being in equilibrium and your spiritual center. Life is simply much more fascinating, engaging, and fruitful when you engage your power of discernment to navigate the situations of your life.

What are you marshaling when you engage your powers of discernment? Your observation of what is so, your intuition, your best intelligence as to how to proceed. As you cultivate a detached observer awareness, you will find it easier not to get sucked into the play around you and the thoughts boomeranging through your attention. You will find it easier and welcoming to create a pause of peace to reawaken your discernment and then proceed with confidence and contentment that you are doing your best.

We are laboring to find and be love in a cold climate. Cold in the sense that our best nature, our experience of the underlying, pervasive oneness of all is wintering. Our better nature, our spiritual insight wants to be brought forth to flow through our life. Daily spiritual practice that you are most comfortable with and committed to will help you awaken and strengthen your discernment as you traverse the day. This will facilitate contentment and the positive feelings that no matter how tough the times or how much you wish for a different coursing of circumstance, you are discerning as best you can how to navigate the current of life.

23 The Prerogatives of Rufflement

You can't remember something you were meant to do. Something feels off in your body, but you have no idea what might be going on. You are running late for an appointment. The meal you ordered and looked forward to is disappointing. You receive a bill that is higher than you expected. Someone says something that only later does not sit right with you. An unpleasant memory from long ago keeps surfacing when least expected and welcome.

Rufflements can crop up at any time. They disturb your equanimity and dismiss your contentment. The quality of your life is compromised as well as your desire and commitment to enjoy the best life possible. The development of your higher mind and your present state of mind will likely dictate the nature of your reaction or response. You may shower imprecations mentally or out loud. You may buttonhole a friend or unsuspecting someone to unload your peeves and maybe extract some agreement as to how unfair life has been treating you. If the corralled offers up some agreement, your bond to them will tighten as your go-to ruffle smoother.

Alternatively, you may realize that when a rufflement casts you down, this is an occasion to nurture your spiritual growth rather than these mental weeds. It is easy to think that these mental disturbances are just part of everyday life and they *are*. The negative mind is merely doing its job of disturbing your calm. Rather than focusing on them, feeding their negative power over you, and attending to them until another one captures your attention, you can identify them as opportunities to vanquish them and enjoy a higher state.

If you wish to elevate your life to an enhanced state of contentment, an enjoyment of blessed beingness, you can honor yourself by acknowledging that presently you are a human being who possesses prerogatives to deal with rufflements as best you can, thus furthering your spiritual evolution. In this context, a prerogative is a special spiritual calling. It is an opportunity to rise above and reclaim yourself as a spiritual being. The experiences that ruffle your state of mind are reminders that your *true life* is infinitely, magnificently grander than your present ego-regarded annoyance.

Humans are God-women and -men, strangers in a strange land. Your life is ordered by the playing out of your destiny karmas, which you can capitalize on as opportunities to strengthen your divine inner connection. Each time you are beset by a rufflement, let it be a reminder of who you truly are beyond the mask of mind and maya *and* the exalted state of being you can regain.

As a spiritual being having a human experience, regardless of how spiritually evolved or unevolved you may deem yourself, you possess the power of discrimination. When your equanimity gets disturbed, you can exercise your discrimination and choose what to do. That is your God-granted prerogative. You possess the prerogative to exercise the will of your higher mind to smooth away, release, or rise above the rufflement. Key factors in truly rising above the disturbances of your mind are awareness and positivity. The question you may want to ask yourself is: *To what extent do I want to be all in to further my spiritual evolution?*

The degree to which you desire to be committed to your spiritual becoming will also correspondingly energize the awakening of your intuition and knowing. Thus, you will be able to discover and employ strategies for dealing with the mind to buttress your composure and reorder your readiness so, rather than going with the negativity, you will have the resolve and confidence to deal with it knowingly.

How to handle rufflements? Here are four approaches that can be experimented with and practiced to allow you to return to your spiritual center. First, when something bothers you, you can decide whether it is an issue meriting action. If it is, do your best to know the most likely approach to resolve it. Rather than rush to resolve it, wait until you feel: *this* is the time to act.

Second, if the rufflement is internal, you can look at the bigger picture and reason with your worrisome self. For instance, how much will this matter in two weeks, a year from now? Then let go and let God.

A third strategy is to deprive the rufflement of your attention and refocus. Just because something unwanted surfaces in your awareness, you do not need to heed it and dwell on it.

Simply redirect your attention and focus on something positive and helpful.

The mind is a potent reactivator. It grooves on well-worn
grooves. If your lower mind is expelling negative thoughts
and memories, remember that this does not serve you. Would
you invite a nasty acquaintance into your home, someone
who has disturbed your peace again and again and eaten your
favorite foods without permission?

The fourth practice is meditation. Until you have tri-
umphed over your mind through meditation, grace, more
effort, and spiritual maturation, your mind is your enemy.
The only way truly to triumph over your mind and make it
your best friend is to meditate daily, immersing yourself in
the Song of God. This Audible Life Stream (called different
names by true Mystics across the centuries) is the all-purpose
antidote to rufflement and every variety of trouble. You will
still have to go through your destiny, processing what you
have sown, but as you meditate and advance, you will be able
to do so increasingly experiencing the inner balm of ease,
contentment, and divine connection.

24 Rich Self-Journeying Fulfillments

On this life journey we are on, we have daily responsibilities that consume our time. We can get estranged from our higher self if we allow them to overtake our days and leave us drained by the time we succumb to sleep. First and foremost, our journey this lifetime is to advance toward God-realization. That is why we have been blessed with birth as a human being.

Aside from our devotion, our spiritual practice, there are gifts of experience that balance us, rebalance us, and evoke our higher mind. These are rich, self-journeying fulfillments that resonate especially with our individual mind-soul being. These fulfillments provide succor on our journey from birth to death and serve to express our innate individual interests.

These practices, activities, and awarenesses are the best of what we are meant to experience in our *daily* life. They feed and enrich the higher mind and are meant to help fulfill this lifetime's journey. They may or may not bring about a communion with the all-pervading divine Spirit. For me, the four most fulfilling practices are meditating, being aware, writing, and reading. Without them, my life would be bereft. Above all else, meditation is the overriding desire of my higher mind. My meager ongoing daily efforts evoke grace, and receptivity to grace is what I crave and treasure.

These four form the foundation of my daily life. They help me fulfill and feel that my precious time here is well served. Frankly, they are the best part of my day-to-day life. A concomitant benefit is that they not only serve to balance, rebalance, and enrich my being, they enable me to know and engage in what else is currently best to balance me. Thus, on any particular day, I may know if and when it serves me to exercise, to engage in honest, unguarded sharing conversation with a friend, or to enjoy a show after a day of intense concentration and completion of tasks.

For another, their foundation might be gardening, grandparenting, playing pickle ball, and quilting. This self-expression is vital. While you are one of the One, here on the physical, you have lived through a shifting kaleidoscope of lives and experiences that have served to form your unique individuality—your native abilities, gifts to contribute, and interests to explore and fulfill yourself. This is all good. Identify, engage in, and bask in your own rich, self-journeying fulfillments, all the time letting yourself be aware that this is who you are best for now, while remembering to remember your true, lasting inner connection to Spirit.

That is delivering contentment. As you engage in theses fulfillments day to day, you are reaping contentment dividends. If events intervene and demand your time and engagement, making you let go of any for a time, that is okay. You can argue with destiny, but that won't help. Your budding, growing awarenesses of who you are this life—your immortal soul with all its beautiful packaging—can allow you to know and accept that this is your self's journey for now. Accept the intervening necessaries, knowing that all things in this world of matter pass, and as much as you'd prefer not to have to go through them, you can also embrace them as an opportunity to be closer to God. No person, no event, no responsibility need have command of your awareness.

When you are able to return to any of your rich, self-journeying fulfilments, you can enjoy them with greater gratitude and reward. Embrace them as meditations that further you on your journey of realizing yourself. They are enlivening preludes on the long journey back to realizing your *true* self. And that is the transcendent, ultimate fulfillment of self- and God-realization.

25 Can You Finesse Your Destiny?

That is a winning question. If we explore it, we enhance our ability to win at life. We may or may not realize that we are puppets, moved by our destiny. We may not know what scenes are waiting for us, nor how we will act despite our best intentions. But we can discover how best we'd like to play each scene, in words and thoughts, and endeavor to be aware and keep practicing.

If you were a struggling actor, you would do everything in your power to win the best parts. Well, the parts have already been assigned. The actors in your scenes will all hit their marks. The weather will sleet or sun on cue. Now you just have to discover how to play your part while simultaneously directing yourself so as not to rack up new karmic debts.

Your part plays out from your *pralabdh* karma (Sanskrit: destiny). Your pralabdh karma is a perfect collocation of your vast reserve of *sinchit* (Sanskrit: reserve) karma accumulated from past lives. Thus, we are saddled with a destiny that we do not know. It is revealed in time, day after day. That is the unspooling of our life. Our parents, relatives, schoolmates, teachers—they all come into our life effortlessly right on time with the niceness and the aggression that is meant to be expressed.

One May day when I was in second grade, I was walking home for lunch side-by-side with a classmate, Shawna, a husky girl with red hair. It was now warm. I took off my jacket and tied it around my waist. Shawna—I still remember her last name—asked me what I was having for lunch. I told her that my mom had saved a leftover hamburger for me. I was having it with catsup and mustard. Oh, and piccalilli! With that word, she stepped in front of me and punched me hard in the face. Boy, that hurt.

Did she think piccalilli is a dirty word? I don't know. All these years later, I still remember the startling punch, the hurt, my hurried walk home, and telling my mother. The events of our life spool out throughout the day. Regardless of whether you want them, they are kept, when all the time, inside, you are craving love and connection. The key to finessing your destiny can be found in two practices.

The first practice is to refrain from actions, speech, and writing that will or could cause suffering. This means being and doing your best to live as your aware self. An element of this is understanding metaphysical laws. For example, if you consume 2,400 chickens during your lifetime—a typical number—you will have to undergo the suffering commensurate to what those 2,400 chickens suffered. You won't have to incarnate 2,400 times as a chicken to be killed and eaten, but that karma you incurred must be paid off.

In a similar vein, writing something to put someone "in

their place," speaking harshly and hurting someone, or helping someone with any expectation of reward all beget reactions. Thoughts are potent. Repeated thoughts lead to actions. Becoming attached to good or bad desires forms grooves in your mind and, at some time in some life in some way, they will be fulfilled. And who can guess what other karmas will be jammed together with them?

What if I had entertained a thirst for revenge against Shawna all these years. She really hurt me physically and emotionally. I did not hit her back. My parents did not call her parents. But if I had fed the desire to get back at her, that would have had consequences.

This may seem all theoretically, pathetically airy-fairy, but if you want to improve your prospects and your lot, it is essential to develop a deeper understanding of metaphysics and act on that for your benefit. Thus, the first side of finessing your destiny—of actually also improving destinies to come—is living with awareness moment to moment so as not to cause suffering or expect results and further cast yourself in plays to come.

What about the suffering you are living through now? What about the diseases, disappointments, and heartaches to come? No matter how good a person you are—and *you are*—your days won't always be sunny and delightfully temperatured to make you sigh and thank your benefic planets (and good aspects in your astrological natal chart). Being alive comes with suffering at appointed times. The way to finesse that suffering is to rise above it with spiritual practice. With the spiritual practice you are most drawn to, you can rise above the dramas, the pains, the unlasting delights, so that you hardly feel the effects of what you are going through. You will still feel the losses and the pain, but at times it will seem as if someone else is going through it. Yes, by devoting yourself to spiritual practice and summoning higher consciousness, in you and around you, you can go through life with an inner smile.

You do not know what the next day or even the next minute will bring. Life can be scary. It is self-defeating to flood your mind with dread or with ongoing absorption in games, shows, fantasies, work, or your problems and those of your loved ones and the world. This play is ending. You will exit the stage at some predetermined time. All the events and the final event will come. Sometimes they will occur without apparent fairness, but you can create an inner contentment, a beatitude, by living in and from the all-benevolent Presence.

That Presence is within you. That Holy Ghost, that Shabd, that Nam is the Sound Current, the Audible God Stream coursing within you. Without it, you would not be alive. It is simply a matter of collecting your ever out-going mind and concentrating at the eye center. Yearning for it, leaning into it evokes grace, awakens your connection with God, helps you detach, and gives you the strength to rise above hurt, conflict, indecision, and suffering. Grace trumps destiny. With spiritual practice, you can finesse your destiny.

26 The Mind Adores

The mind adores self-interest, calculation, money, feeling secure, consuming fantasy, animalistic urges, tasty dishes, the tried and true, clichés, opinions, being right, being religious, rituals, winning, feel-good charity, complication, simplicity, game shows, birthday cake, gossip, secrets, fast boats, gurgling babies, hot fudge sundaes, clean and complete kerplops, fresh towels, new cars, classic cars, rubbernecking, bigfoot sightings, hope, self-invention, self-pity, feeling lucky, being occupied, patriotism, hating politicians, hating governments, conspiracy theories, getting even, getting drunk, pissing, showboating, morning-after cures, beach reads, plans for the evening, good news, having lots of news, talking a blue streak, sanctimonious people being shown up, guessing right, dressing up, drag, old clothes, smells that take you back to a better time, keepsakes of a dearly departed, a good cry (well-deserved), bonbons, keeping it together, losing it, simple pleasures, being appreciated, being adored, thinking.

27   The Soul Adores

The soul adores God.

28 The Illusion of Success

How do you define success? Is it finding your soul partner, your forever love? Is it making a big difference; for instance, moving the world toward sustainability? Is it making an amazing amount of money? Or might it be finding a clean, safe shelter for a few nights? Is it enjoying all the peak experiences you can? Or is it finding your purpose in life and fulfilling it?

If it is the latter, let's first investigate why you are here. Why were you born? Was it biological happenstance? Our species' imperative to propagate and perpetuate our genes? Evolved humans who have achieved true mystical knowing would tell you that a culling of karmas from your past lives formed your destiny this lifetime. You were born into a particular concatenation of circumstances with people entering the scenes of your life, interacting with you, and leaving at their appointed times.

Have you ever wondered what actions and reactions you committed in the past and will in the days to come that will add to your load of karmic debt? That massive mountain of debt, a smidgen of which will be culled to form your next life's trajectory, will keep you coming back in the physical again and again and again.

You were born after a seemingly innumerable number of lives. Finally, now as a human, you have a precious opportunity. That is God-realization.

The human form while alive is the only vehicle for embarking on this transformation. Rather than being a cow or dog or a devoted person of faith, perhaps before you were born this lifetime you were an angel or enjoyed a heaven for the equivalent of tens of thousands of earth years. As either entity, you were deprived of the opportunity of advancing your awakening to achieve the ultimate success, which is forever Wonder.

We are trapped in a constantly alluring labyrinth, unlike the mythological one that King Minos of Crete commanded to be built for the Minotaur, who had the body of a man and the head and tail of a bull. Our labyrinth is aboveground, belowground, in the air, and outer space. Our world is replete with endless attractions and diversions and also sufferings from which we try to escape (if we are so inclined). All but a few of us are *unaware* that we are caught in a labyrinth. We may rail against people, injustice, our lot in life. We may bemoan what we deem to be failures—personal, familial, political—but the real failure is the failing to take advantage of our human birth. True success is escaping the labyrinth of these lower, alien worlds and the returning to Home.

We have suffered through myriad lives rising above lives in slime; gaining movement on earth, in water, then flight;

and finally, becoming an animal. After innumerable times being eaten or slaughtered to relish the palate of humans, we evolve to humankind (not devoid of reptilian or animalistic tendencies). Now is our chance to realize everlasting success. When will we have this opportunity again?

Listen, dear friend, if you are reading or listening to this part, you have attained a juncture in your journey where you can proceed with realizing your divine Self. You can retain your goals in the world *and* heed the call of seeking the true success. Yes, continue to strive for and achieve your worldly goals and desires—ideally while inculcating an attitude of detachment. Regardless how noble and fulfilling they are, after you achieve them, an emptiness will set in—your soul is still longing for Oneness. Those achievements are not yours. Even if you end up in history for magnificent or foul deeds, your consciousness will not be there to revel in that illusory success.

Real success is lasting. It's not a mirage, a number of likes or hearts on a screen that readily get supplanted. We *are* meant to help our fellow human beings and creatures, and that person (or animal) to whom you give of yourself will be helped and grateful to whatever extent they are, but that success cannot be taken with you.

Being a human now means you have won the best lottery. This level of existence is impermanent. Change is the order of time. If you take stock of your life, you may wonder whether you can progress toward the ultimate, lasting success. Yes, you can. Why not? Remember, effort evokes grace (an inswelling of God's mercy). And it is God's grace that allows effort.

You can strive toward your personal goals, knowing that if you achieve them, how satisfying yet fleeting that sensation of success may be. Also know that commanding desires—long-lurking and new—may direct you to another stage; it may feel like a new life, percolating with rejuvenating possibilities. We are each an actor in this play with a limited run. We are meant to move from stage to stage in various roles, achieving whatever success comes our way.

If you feel called to achieve true success, that is, actually becoming LoveSource, that forever Life for which we were born to long, just keep returning to this desire and make it your lodestar.

29 Disenchantment Comes Easily

The lures and allures of the world are meant to pull you into their embrace. They capture your attention. They excite with their promise. They consume your time; at times your money; ultimately your desire.

Then you are left with an emptiness that caws for being filled. Your attention flies about until a false sparkle catches your mind's eye and then it alights upon the next shiny object of desire.

We live in a world of enchantments that readily cast their spell. The mind loves to be ensorcelled. For it is alone, cast down from its home, regardless of the love it thinks it has. With the attachment of its attention, we gain forgetfulness, relief. A deceptive, ephemeral union salves the pain of being cast about in the world from one experience to the next.

We live in a fantasy world, a perpetual season of spells whirling about, catching us in their vortexes. Any new or familiar dust devil of a spell lifts us up, takes us for a spin, then it dissipates and we hit cold ground. Hard disenchantment.

Then you may dive again into your device or whichever

spell-master seizes you. And so, your life goes on—enchantment followed by disenchantment. What can prize away the dullness that keeps coming and can drive you crazy? Disenchantment comes easily. And comes easily again and again. Will you ever come to and notice a bifurcation of your path?

The well-trod path—the one of easy movement and familiar promise and expected pleasure surely is the one leading you further into the world. The other path leads to the seeking of a solution. A resolution of enchantment-disenchantment and your chance of transcendence to seek the real and true disenchantment—the Everlasting.

There is a way out, a soul-affirming path to become clear and rise above the spells. The outer and inner steps on that path are uniquely your own. Eventually, you will want to find a spell dissolver, a true Truth teller. Do not trust your mind. Discover your higher knowing. You can follow your best outer path as long as you concurrently access and follow that inner knowing.

Have faith in grace and your receptivity. Know that the necessary faith is yours; it comes when you feel you have reached a dead-end and there is nothing more. But there is. Even though you may not know just what you want to seek—bliss, everlasting love?—your quest will grow, you will see buds and blossoms along your way, and your quest will bear fruit. If not this lifetime, then the next. If not the next, then the one after that. Have faith, you will find you will be found.

30 The Decrement of Time

What is keeping you from awakening from the enchantment of time? Many of us remain unaware of the decrement of time and labor under its misconceptions. (Decrement means the quantity lost by gradual waste.) We remain oblivious of these misconceptions.

The first main misconception is: your time is not slipping away. The decrement of time over minutes, days, months, years is so stealthy and steady that your mind and the world easily keep you inattentive to what truly matters. The way of the world is to capture your attention with all its wiles and usurp your most precious commodity—the exact time you've been allotted this lifetime. Rich men and rulers on their death beds would willingly have given everything to gain more breaths. Saints through the ages say that your number of breaths is fixed at birth.

"I have all the time in the world." People in their eighties believe that they will live well into their nineties. Where is their guarantee? People in their forties and fifties look forward to their golden years of retirement. They believe that they possess oodles of blooming acres of time. But a tumor, an accident could prove them wrong at any time. "Time waits for no man." Or woman, or non-binary while the decrement of time proceeds inexorably.

Another main misconception that enchants people is: it's okay to waste time. Their enchantment encourages them to believe that much of the time they deserve to do whatever pleases them. They think (if, in fact, they do) that wasting time is without consequence. The consequence is that you forfeit the opportunity to proceed toward a contentment of bliss beyond your imagination. Right now, this is your most critical choice: either wander in the country of discontent and superficial contentment, or seek the realms of rising joy.

Unaware that their life continues to seep away from them, when pressed to finish something, people exclaim, "I'm running out of time." That's true, but all the time you are running out of time. When someone—a friend, a loved one—meets their end unexpectedly, some will pronounce with dismay that their life was "cut short." It just seems that way. On a higher plane of consciousness and reality, their lifetime reached its ordained end.

One of the ways we continue to be spellbound by the enchantment of time is we keep thinking that all kinds of things need to get done and pleasures experienced. We fail to distinguish between what is meritorious and what is enjoyable, or merely pleasant. Enchanted by the material world, oblivious of the decrement of time, we fail to take responsibility for our spiritual evolution and achievement of ultimate, perfect contentment. Our mind directs us with never-ending insistences.

What is merely pleasant and diverting allows you to get lost in whatever captures the fancy of your mind. Your lower mind is in league with time, keeping you from seeking the door to eternity. For those who have found it, the enchantment of time exerts such a powerful pull that they forget and fail to knock.

If you are able to be in touch with your inborn sense of discrimination, you could exercise it and learn to discriminate as to what is unnecessary and unhelpful in your daily life and what is truly good for the ongoing awakening and realization of your higher being, your true self. All the while fulfilling your worldly duties. Exercising your enlightened sense of discrimination includes the development of higher moral qualities, among them, honesty, positivity, generosity of spirit.

To endeavor to awaken further from the enchantment of time, do your best to sense the presence of God. God (and even your unwitting expression of incipient godliness) is beyond time.

31 The Rewards of Disenchantment

Is this all there is?

Have you ever wondered that? And felt there must be something more? By "this" is meant life as you presently know and experience it. If you really look at material objects—a spoon, a table, a wall—truly gaze—a certain unreality to them becomes apparent.

Yes, you can touch them and register the feel of them. As time passes, they will pass away, not only from your life but from their current form as well and be something else. Think of ancient civilizations that were considered advanced, beyond atrophy. Now so long gone that archaeologists will find nary a shard.

We are living in a material world that hides the abiding reality of the divine. If God exists and we are serving as experiential manifested projections of that omnipresent, invisible creative force, certainly you can say we have been given a raw deal. Blame the enchantment on God. Blame it on your mind. Consign the blame to all the stuff in the world that excites your passions. It is all the Will. *And* in concert with the Will is God's grace always to awaken further, to cast off the spells, to evolve spiritually a little more and long to be one of the chosen to gain *disenchantment*.

What does disenchantment mean? It means realizing yourself—that is, achieving the exalted consciousness in which you experience that your actual self is Self, a particle, an immortal spark of the eternal, infinite nameless Being. Thus, disenchantment is a process of spiritual evolution. If that is the trajectory of your consciousness, rather than allowing your mind free rein to get further entangled, heedlessly pursuing desire after desire adding to your vast reserve of karmas, consciously discriminate what does not authentically serve you. You can design your days to support awakening and growing your awareness of God. Believe in the heart of your soul that, though this is a slow process, it is imbued with encouraging synchronicity and grace when you least expect it.

People worship the divine in all manner of ways. That is good. Faith is a critical component of our advancement and success to truly realizing ourselves. While we are still here, alive and observant, any feeling that is transcendent, deliciously inviting, soul-awakening—seize it. Love that feeling. Remember it and remember to remember it. Regard and honor that feeling as an open sesame. Let it be the open sesame to the end of your enchantment.

When you begin to understand metaphysical truths, life begins to make sense and your desire to seek truth becomes a thrilling experience. You may be familiar with the saying attributed to Pierre Teilhard de Chardin and at times to G. I. Gurdjieff: "We are not human beings having a spiritual experience; we are spiritual beings having a human experience." To function as humans on this physical plane, we must be stationed in a physical body. When we are not on this Earth, we exist elsewhere.

We still have our mind and are experiencing what we must—for instance, reviewing our recent life on Earth, suffering intensely for hurtful actions we committed, or enjoying spiritual education. Or we are preparing for our next earthly sojourn, according to what is being utilized from our storehouse of karmas, or we may be out and right back in a human or other species, dormant for a time, awaiting birth. It is quite individual.

When we left our purely divine existence, our original Home, and ventured down into the mental planes, our soul was joined with a mind. Typically, it is the mind we refer to when we think, *I*, but that is an illusion. Dwelling on the physical plane, we have committed action after action, allowing our senses, our pleasures, our ego drives to take over. Desire has driven our life trajectory life after life and kept us coming back, as the bonds of enchantment have grown stronger and stronger, and apparently invincible.

As unhappy as we can be with things we don't like, as much as we can enjoy our short-lived pleasures, we (that is, our mind) always wants. The mind has succumbed fully to its enchantment. Even if we devote ourselves to the beneficial achievement of good works, that laudable, lofty enterprise is an attachment that binds us further to keep coming back to enjoy the fruits of our actions.

Unless you happen to be a very evolved soul or Saint

who has incarnated here for a special purpose, you are likely saddled with an obstinate, powerful mind that wants what it wants and continues to enslave your soul, keeping it captive as your mind gets further lost in the world and taking you further away from your true divine Home, as well as the mind's original sphere in the mental plane.

Listen, dear friend, on this long, long journey, of which our current life is but a nano-flicker, it is ever so easy to become disheartened. Peggy Lee lent a special world-weariness speaking the lyrics in the song "Is That All There Is?" Written by Jerry Lieber and Mike Stoller, it tells of an adult relating a series of events in her life when she was a little girl— seeing her house catch on fire, going to the circus and, when she was older, falling in love with a boy, only to have him go away. Again and again she sings the refrain, "Is that all there is?" And if it is, her response is to "break out the booze."

Yes, when disappointment catches and crushes you, it is ever so easy to break out the booze or lose yourself in whatever your mind runs to and gloms on to. But when you have the feeling that something is missing—ah, that is a gift. Seize that feeling. Treasure it. Discover its significance. Might it be the longing of your soul for God?

Once you are aware that you are living under a state of enchantment, you can go about your day observing how the world and your desires pull you away from yourself. You can practice being more mentally detached from the outcomes of your actions and neutral about what happens and remember that it is the Will. This growing knowing of how you are tricked and sucked in by what is outside of you is a blessing and a sign that you are awakening further. You might begin to wonder: If I become fully awakened and disenchanted, what could that be like?

The rewards of becoming fully disenchanted are glorious, a life of consummate contentment, transcendence of the small ego-bound self to live in true love. But as you proceed with your meditation on the Sound Current (having been initiated by a living Master), your state of knowingness expands naturally. True intuition comes readily more often. Your awareness blooms so you increasingly feel a Presence around and within you. Loneliness is a forgotten malady. You love your company, its stillness and fullness.

This does not mean you shut yourself off as a hermit. You fulfill your personal, familial, and social responsibilities with less resistance and more good cheer because of your detached attitude and inner contentment. You serve yourself and others better. You are more in tune to express your better nature and you radiate a peace so that most people feel more at ease and peaceful around you.

This is all well and good as you meditate daily and take that wakefulness with you, ideally appreciative that grace is always available and effort begets more grace and enhanced receptivity. In reality, you are likely aware of but a smidgen of grace that is lovingly and perfectly working through you to end your enchantment.

This is but a little about your in-process awakening. What can be expressed about what it is like to achieve complete disenchantment? Only those who have freed themselves of their mind's mastery can give hints. For seekers who are journeying back Home, the rewards are first the brilliant journey of beauty and wonders ascending through the heavenly realms. You have fulfilled God's experience via your soul of manifested life in innumerable forms of life across the creation. It is liberation of your soul from the outgoing, unsatisfiable mind. The icing, and the utterly delectable "cake," is never having to suffer again for the consequences of all the misdeeds you committed in the past—for your meditation and best efforts of immersion in the Sound Current with the grace of forgiveness has cleared your karmic reserve.

The ultimate reward? If your Guide is fully realized, merged in the divine, then they can be your most intimate, trustworthy companion, guiding your inner mystical progression of consciousness *all the way back*. They can take you through the great darkness that is impenetrable to those who have not crossed and return you to your original being of unalloyed bliss and wonder and love.

32 The Concatenation of Meritorious Immersions

Imagine that you could bathe in a celestial lake. Freed of all your physical aches and limitations, when your soul immerses in the living ambrosia, your remaining impurities are cleansed, the water of life rejuvenates you as never before, and you rejoice in the realization of your magnificent divine nature.

Gaining surcease from the troubles and strife of worldly life—an imaginary fancy? Others have succeeded. Why not you?

In the meantime, you possess the self-knowing to rise above much, neutralizing the frustrating, the unpleasant, the down-pulling—whatever you have encountered each day. For instance, you've had a tough day, particularly dealing with a recalcitrant bureaucracy or business that has unfairly ripped you off. Perhaps barely intelligible, misunderstanding representatives have sapped your energy and time. You had to call forth a supreme effort to resolve the issue and be able to proceed to the next priority of your life.

In your favor, that day is done and you have a free evening. You have done your best this day of challenges to be patient and kind to achieve an honest, benevolent outcome. Now you can let go. If you are moved to, prepare an appealing meal for yourself or others, spicing it with love. Savor each bite (regardless of how it turned out). Later, if you are planning to relax and watch shows, listen to music or podcasts, or engage in a hobby, choose those that will soothe and uplift your state of mind and allow you to experience beauty, enjoy yourself, and feel good.

If you were aware of and attended to an intuitive feeling and chose well, you will feel renewed, positive, content, for you infused merit into your evening. The practice of engaging in positive, uplifting pastimes that reorient your state of mind is something to recall and engage in not only on your down, trying days, but also your so-so days and good days.

Day after day, when you are raising your vibration and awakening your enthusiasm for better, higher states of mind, you are instilling merit in your being. Meritorious intentions and deeds make a difference throughout your life and across lives. Engage in them ideally with no thought of self-glorification and reward. Meritorious selfless intentions and deeds further your spiritual evolution and invite divine favor. For instance, goodness blooms when you reach out to a friend who has been ill or experienced a trauma by calling or visiting to genuinely see and ask how they are doing.

Meritorious recreations for yourself could include being kind to yourself, to all living beings, and to our environment. Second, whenever you catch yourself going negative, be positive. Let go of negative worrisome thoughts whenever they crop up and foster positive thoughts and beliefs. Third, when you do not know "what next," ask within for guidance. Throughout the day ask how best to be with God. That may be merely an unknown or an inarticulate feeling, but you are moving toward evoking the Presence and making yourself more akin to God.

Thus, meritorious movements for and toward God include invoking and evoking the Presence within and around you as best you can. That power is within you, is the true you, covered up by your outward desires and mental activity. You simply need to build on confident faith that, with grace, your soul opens and your higher mind is made aware.

The practice that truly abets and attracts the Presence is remembrance throughout the day of God. The grace is always there. It is merely a question of your receptivity. Acknowledge that you have spent a seeming eternity of forgetting and getting further embroiled in the creation life after life, taking you further away from where you once belonged. And have faith that, regardless of whether you believe you lived so many times before, the concatenation of meritorious immersions life after life has already or will prepare you for the ultimate immersion.

The ultimate immersion is the connection to, meditation on, and listening to the mystical Sound Current that is resounding within your concentrated higher consciousness. This is the divine expression of God you possess. It is the camino real within you to brilliantly beautiful and blissful sights and experiences on the mystic path. Access is gained by a living Guide who initiates you into the practice of meditation on the Sound Current.

Perhaps your desire to withdraw your mental and soul currents and go within has not become a critical priority, and the pulls of strictly worldly engagement and the ongoing satisfaction of your panoply of pleasures still hold sway over you. That is as it is. The time may come when the pull to within is irresistible and the aching of your soul for communion is finally registered and must be heeded.

The concatenation of meritorious immersions across myriad human lives may have reached the tipping point and you are primed to seek the all-embracing love that your soul knew and was. But now you are tramping through time—albeit with keener awareness—and you may resent God's adventure on your behalf. That Power may maintain that you started with free will. Ha! That was no match for the pull of the senses and the ego's ongoing ascendancy, getting you further embroiled so your karmic debts imprisoned you in time and consigned you to life after life after life.

Whatever you have been through, each birth in a physical world wrapped you in the caul of forgetting. But now you may be dipping into incomparable sweetness. Regardless of how distracted you may be day in, day out, the sweet aches of your soul keep breaking through to your awareness this lifetime, for you have enacted meritorious intentions, deeds, and immersions across many lives. You have been spiritualized in all the ways you needed to be. The completed effect of these immersions is that your higher mind has become predominant over your base mind a majority of the time. And now you may be ready to focus on and commit to attaining your complete contentment and being relieved of all the debts you have accumulated.

This is surely possible. With God's grace and will, inevitably it is finding and following your true path of *bhakti*, of devotion, to realize your true nature and Home, which has been awaiting your return since time immemorial.

33 The Inevitability of Desserts

For me and, I believe, for many others, dessert is the most anticipated course of a meal. I love the sweetness, the confluence of flavors, especially when I enjoy two fantastic flavors of ice cream surrounding a vegan cupcake. Then I really bask in the yumminess of the dessert. Some children, who were raised without real love but who could have sweets—a cookie, an ice cream, a shaved-off piece of cake when no one was around and which hopefully would not be noticed—those desserts were a filler for love. That's why people take their sweet tooth into adulthood and to the grave.

Humans have six primary tastes: astringent, bitter, pungent, salty, sour, and sweet. Sweet is the dominant taste we possess. What is the traditional way to celebrate birthdays across many cultures? To serve a birthday cake, that treasured dessert that comes for you but once a year. It could be a pie, a sweet bun, a pudding, but that dessert is special.

The sweet taste promotes compassion, peacefulness, and love. If you buy or prepare a dessert for yourself or others, this is a way of giving solace. It is an expression of kindness. If your life is emotionally barren, or your job and/or struggles to subsist are tough, it is particularly gratifying to have your birthday remembered and acknowledged with a sweet dessert. Especially if you do it for yourself and that was your sole possibility.

Let's hope that you have that one day a year—if not many more—in which you are remembered and appreciated. What about the other 364 days of the year? How sweet, how kind will they be? Have you been and will you be besieged by so much that it feels as if it is too much? You may ask—especially if you reach the point of exasperation—*why is this happening to me?* It may be one thing after another or too much altogether—the breakdown of something, a frustrating glitch amongst too many demands on you, a broken commitment, a mean act, a failure of others to extend elementary decency.

When someone you are disappointed with because their behavior has been hurtful, and then at some point they get their comeuppance, you may think: *they're getting their just deserts.* But you only experienced an element of their subjective totality, not to mention their entire objective truth. For the most, people remain prisoners of their past. Acting out their destiny, they are puppets who are not always well-meaning. Your judgment does not serve you. It sours and bitters your mind. What about when a disappointment befalls you? Do you think: *I'm getting my just deserts?* If you read, listen to, or watch the news, the traumas and suffering reported can feel spirit-sickening, unless you rise above it. We seem to be lurching irreversibly into darker and deadlier times.

Yes, the world can easily feel altogether violent and unforgiving. What dreaded deed might next visit you and all those whom you should wish good? A sweet life can seem like a naïve hope, a ridiculous dream, a capricious promise. But, the sweetest of life can be inevitable. How? The key? It is the inner knowing and faith that you can win an existence that is the sweetest of sweetness.

If you have ever enjoyed the ineffable grace and goodness of being in the company of a true Saint, one reality that will ease through your being is the pure sweetness they exude. Once you experience it, you know it is far superior to anything you could ever taste or have in this world. Saints speak of the inevitability of an eternal state of being that is beyond our best imaginings, but it is a continuous course of love and wonder.

By completing your individual course of duty in this physical life and, most importantly, by following the instructions of a living Saint, including daily devotion to meditation, that is how you can achieve this eternal dessert and it will be your just desert. *Desert*, distinguished from desserts and arid land, is related to deserve. Thus meditating, your at-oneing with God, is reversing your movements away from LoveSource during your lives on the lower planes of existence and ultimately bestows the grace and atonement of what you now deserve, reunion with God.

If you realize a true desire for God alone, if you return again and again to that desire of devotion, it is inevitable that your being and consciousness will purify and ultimately become the sweetness that is complete exalted contentment.

34 The Repetition of a Signifier for Our Constant Conductor

The mind loves repetition—thinking thought after thought, experiencing sensation after sensation. Thinking and imaging endless variations of the same concern, show, rejoinder to an unwelcome remark—it's all repetition. Does your mind ever long to be still? Sure, if you're tired or stressed, you may just want to lose yourself in a favorite show. But the dialogue and scenes of the show are being repeated in your mind as you absorb them and often the next day as your mind replays them, distracting you from whatever could be better focused on. "As we think, so we become." This is attributed to the Buddha. Our thoughts give rise to actions. As we act, we create the destinies of our future lives. Our destinies are culled from the effects of our actions and our attachments, the desires that scratch lasting grooves in our mind and congeal as karma, borne by us until they are paid off.

Since the mind is always spewing thoughts and scenes—an encounter at work, the violence of a scene in a show, a remembered hurt, a retort, an anxious stream of what-ifs—why not override the scattering negative, down-pulling stream of thoughts to which, in truth, you are a slave?

The elusive self remains hidden by mental coverings. Our mind orders our being. Our thoughts are our reality, and our attachment to mental patterns and apprehension of sensual experiences prevent us from gaining a consciousness that is freer, happier. We remain incognizant of our precious soul, except for those mysterious bitter and sweet longings, for something unnameable, for love, for something that will fill and complete us for good. That is the soul breaking through to our mental awareness.

Throughout time, humans have sensed a greater power, a pervasive creative force and given it many names. In cultures that have risen and disappeared, true Saints, perfect Masters (but also false prophets), philosophers, religious leaders, kings, queens, and nomads have named that highest being, that transcendent creative force they have believed in, sensed, experienced, or actually rejoined. God, Goddess, the Lord, the Father, Supreme Being, YHWH, Jehovah, Elohim, Deus, Allah, Hu, Bhagavan, Khu, Anami. These are but a few of the myriad names given by some on our planet to revere the nameless One.

The nameless One is the creative force that issued forth in mystical, omnipotent, glorious Sound and Light as the Audible Life Stream to create multiplicity. As that Sound Current issued forth, the realms of existence consisted of lesser spirit; mind came into being and ultimately physical stuff—animate and inert, from the plant kingdom to the life form that could worship, revere, and ponder the mystery of life and God—human beings.

Each soul is one of the multitudinous in the infinite multiverses of creation. Human beings have been granted the most precious gift: the primordial creative element of ether (*akash* in Sanskrit) with the spiritual senses of listening to and seeing (*surat* and *nirat*) the Sound Current. The catch for most of us now is that our minds have become predominant, so ruled by the physical senses and the constant goings-on in our mind and the world that we are too scattered (except for some) to hear an echo of an echo of that most glorious Sound. Yet even in our quiet moments, we may notice something akin to the sound of the sea in a seashell. The divine Ocean is ever present. But each one of us is one of the multitudinous symphonies of soul. Ultimately, we can consciously rejoin the real mystical symphonies that become more glorious, more enrapturing as we ascend back into the realms of purer and purer spirit (with less and less admixture of mind and matter).

The simplest way to entreat a conscious connection is to repeat a name internally. That omniscient life force is always here—it's our attention that is elsewhere. You can reconduct the outgoing mind by engaging in the repetition of a signifier for our nameless One. Repetition is the saying over and over in our minds, with concentration and love, a word or words or phrase that for you signifies the ultimate eternal Source of love and creative expression. The repetition of your signifier can signify the transcendent experience of mystic reality even as you progress through your allotment of days while you occupy your current body.

For the One who knows all your needs and what you must go through this current lifetime, why not ask for that One alone? This is the One whose all-pervasive Presence conducts the play of all life. You can begin to collect your attention and life force by repeating a signifier for our Constant Conductor. You can repeat any word or words that most strongly resonate with you. If religious names and past experiences carry unwelcome baggage, choose your own. The main thing to resonate with and intend is that this repetition is a spiritual act of *remembrance* of your true Home, for which your soul *longs*.

Why Constant Conductor? It is neutral and descriptive. That Power is the all-dynamic, creative Current that issues from the limitless, nameless Source of all. It *is* the Supreme Eternal Life, the only reality that exists forever, regardless of its infinite expressions throughout its creations.

If that Supreme Being is all love, perhaps it is more keen that you can know for you to turn within and call for that love with your heart, summoning the realization of your connection by focusing your mind and engaging in the repetition of a signifier that you embrace as yours and that can focus and heighten your awareness.

Repetition is the key to success. Bringing your mind back again and again to repeat a signifier for God is the essential effort that evokes grace and the salubrious flowing through the day. Yes, we get to struggle; yes, your thoughts will persistently intercede, but the known and unknown rewards are magnificent. Repetition is required to subdue the mind and to reprogram it from its negative tracks. Persons who have fully realized their spirituality are masters of their minds. Repetition is the foundation of spiritual practice.

What are some of the many other profound benefits of the repetition of a signifier for our Constant Conductor? Your repetition overrides thoughts that scatter your attention and take you away from your spiritual center, and which otherwise would take you on a downward spiral often of negativity that prevents you from being conscious, on purpose, and making best use of your limited time. Repetition stills and quiets the mind to nurture the clear thinking that serves you.

Repetition of a name or names that feels right for you and spiritually potent brings you into the present, simultaneously heightening awareness and expanding your consciousness so you exist consciously in your new now.

As soon as you are aware that thoughts have hijacked your repetition, refocus your mind and immerse yourself in your beloved signifier with full concentration. Again and again, thoughts will pop up and take you down one weedy path, then another, and another. Your mind with its ever-issuing thoughts has been your dominant power and lord for ages. But you have will that you can summon and exercise. Simply return to your focus and resume your repetition.

This repetition will allow your higher knowing to come through. Inspired ideas, things you'd best attend to (but would otherwise fail to), priorities and answers will come through in your awareness.

Naturally, when you are concentrating on your repetition, be in a safe place; for example, don't lose yourself in repetition while you are driving. Allow yourself to realize that by being in your repetition, you are furthering your journey, the best journey, to realizing your true self, your soul.

The repetition of a signifier for our Constant Conductor spiritualizes you. It is transformative. Think of your mind as consisting of myriad twentieth-century phonograph records, those vinyl flat discs inscribed with a spiral groove that when the needle of the record player's arm was placed on the periphery of the groove while the turntable turned, would produce sound. If the vinyl record became scratched or too much dust adhered, it easily became a broken record causing the same phrase of a tune or scratchy sounds to repeat over and over. Our minds overrule us by playing old tunes again and again—often variations of a theme, like what you'd say to the person who made that cutting remark, but you won't so your rejoinder plays over and over. Our thoughts track reck-lessly along well-worn grooves, but another record will read-ily fall into place to relish the attention of our mind's needle, regardless of our intention and will.

The repetition of a signifier for our Constant Conductor *cleanses* and *erases* the grooves of our thought patterns and fills them with awakening of the higher mind, receptivity for grace and upliftment, and connectivity to the divine Presence within. It neutralizes our spewing thoughts—often anxious, fearful, and stuck in the regretted, hurtful past or the dreaded future. Those misleading, unnecessary thoughts are replaced with a clean slate. A slate that advances the liberation of your soul, which, though still dominated by the mind, con-ducts your attention to the Source. Further, your repetition conjoins your attention with that Omniscience. This is your call to the nameless One, that omnisciently loves your turning within, asking for help, rousing your receptivity to grace and the strength to summon your best efforts to get through life's challenges. The Omniscience knows your every need, your destiny this lifetime that you must fulfill.

Regardless of your destiny, always prompt yourself to turn humbly within for grace and mercy. The most transformative repetition is that given and empowered by a *living* Guide who has merged their soul with the Oversoul. If you have no pull to connect with a Guide, a Teacher, that's fine. If you do, your repetition is a powerful call to be found and initiated into the realities that await you within the higher realms of existence.

Saints have said that not a leaf stirs without God's will. That creative power, remember, is flowing in and through everything, manifesting its will (as the laws of each realm are observed—like karma). It is the conductive reality of everything in existence, regardless of the projected form it assumes. The celestial music and lights throughout the created realms of being are all expressions of our Constant Conductor. The creative Current that resides in and animates you can be withdrawn—when you die, but also while you are alive. On a finer, more spiritual plane, your awareness can experience a higher reality.

If you have been given repetition by a realized Guide, when you rise within and behold the mystical radiant form of your Guide, your repetition is complete. Once you connect and rejoin the Current that evolves you higher and higher, you are being conducted along the Current to more glorious, rarefied states of being. This is the journey our Constant Conductor has readied for you—ultimately leaving the mind behind to rise and rise, realize your soul's divinity, and once again *be* the Infinite.

35 Grist to One's Will

Life can be fraught with uncertainties, jostling desires, strivings, difficulties, your screw-ups, and those of others. Gosh, life can be tough. Rather than dwell on these botherations, you can focus on the available higher pleasure that you can access.

It is all too easy for you to focus on what the mind deems to be *not right*. It's easy to feel that you're just grist, that each day you are ground through the mill of life, left as chaff for the wind. Regardless if you are partnered, in a family, active in a community, it's easy to feel alone. Unsupported, at a loss, of no matter to anyone.

Listen, dear friend, you are never alone. You can realize a spiritual connection within your being. Regardless of whether you believe in a higher Being, an all-pervading, all-knowing force of love and mercy, you possess an innate faculty of worship. You can worship regardless of what you believe or question. To worship is not to ask for things. Worship is a profound focus of awareness and openness that lightens your load, uplifts your spirit, and gladdens your heart. Worship is an act of sacred connection. In worship, you are simply one human being turning your awareness within to be with the Oneness. You are offering your true self to be one with the Oneness.

With this selfless act, you surrender. Instead of forging about in your thoughts, with this selfless act you become grist to One's will. With this humble act of offering yourself and seeking connection, you relieve yourself of the burdens that make your life fraught with troubles and discontent. This eases your mind and your life, and elevates you to a spiritual field around you that affords an experience of the Oneness.

Worship is both the grist and the mill though which the ego is ground down and your attention is transmuted to the divine. Worship is part and parcel of the divine plan. *The Oneness worships its being though us.* With focused, ardent concentration, with letting go of your small self, you are oneing with the Oneness that pervades all.

Grist to One's will is the idea that you submit your will to the divine will. "Let go and let God" conveys freedom and flow. The act of worship lifts you above your insistent I-ness and my-ness. In true, guileless worship, you let yourself be subsumed in the Oneness. Worship entails no set prayers, props, or rituals—it is a spontaneous meditation that aligns you with the Presence within you (and also around you).

Who can fathom the will of the Oneness? We are so self-willed that we remain blind to this play of love in which we have been cast. We've committed myriad acts that have later written for us scenes of suffering but also discovery and joy. We reap what we have sown. The law of action and reaction, cause and effect, is the will of the Oneness.

The infinite play of creation is the way the Oneness emanates its infinite being through us. When we focus with devoted sincerity our awareness within even when we are looking out or moving about, our worship becomes the grist that ennobles us and enables us to rise above the illusion of this play. When we worship amidst the ongoingness of life, the chaff from our ego falls away and kernels of love and awareness are multiplied divinely with the love-charged Oneness. Now, when needs summon your attention, you can engage in the enterprises of life freed of your chagrins.

As we become more aware of and experience the higher joy awaiting us, we begin to know when to worship. Until we are masters of our minds, we will remain separate, and as slaves of the mind, that is the will we likely *think* we follow. If we are even that aware. At the mercy of the mind, we forge headstrong through our days without feeling one with the will of the Oneness. Following impulse after impulse, thought after thought, we continue to be cast in a chaff storm of forgetfulness. *And*, all this time, now, the mystical sound and light of the One can be sought with awareness and transmute you. But we are buried in the storms of the world when we believe the storms demand our attention.

When you are aware of blindly following your mind's will—its insistent urgencies—remember that you need not stumble and drift heedlessly in a desert of aloneness. You have the will and the capacity to engage in a sacred act whenever you wish. You can worship, seeking the Oneness, seeking a way to truly merge with the Oneness. Summoning the Oneness within you, you automatically become aligned with the will of the One and go about your times here in a beatitude of equilibrium, happy and content. Being less separate and ever more aware of the Oneness of which you are.

36 Unifying the Selflessness

Most of us suffer from an aggrieved case of self-fullness. This is the dilemma of the self. The self we are mainly conscious of and identify with is the wanting self. It is the ego, radiating through the spheres of mind from the lower to the higher mind, which is driven by desire, succumbing to impulses and thoughts that dominate our attention. We are trapped in our wanting self, and if and when a want is satisfied, that satisfaction soon seeps away, leaving us to suffer from the flatness. This self-fullness of want, of never experiencing *lasting* satisfaction, keeps us from experiencing true contentment.

Even when we're glad and satisfied during and immediately after a good meal or movie or sex, it is short-lasting and all too soon an unfulfilled desire has us. The mind that masquerades as the self has us at its mercy as we identify with its thoughts, desires, and sense attractions. This life is a lone merry-go-round ride, as we ride up and down to the carny music of our mind, never getting off, not realizing our actual disorientation.

The antidote to the discontent we suffer from self-fullness is selflessness. We may experience selflessness while being of

service, feeling or expressing empathy, and while losing ourselves in creative work and expression. During these experiences we may rise in awareness to the unifying field that
permeates all existence, the God Current. The purer we are,
the closer we are to a greater awareness of the God Current.
God Current is simply another name for the Supreme
LoveSource, the very stuff that is life and creates existence.

We can more fully realize an ongoing state of unifying
awareness when in our meditation we concentrate our mind
and soul currents at the eye center and withdraw our awareness from the physical realm. Meditating on the God Current,
traversing the inner regions with a realized Master, becoming purer, ascending higher to finer realms of successively
less mind and greater spirit, we can ultimately be purified to
the state where we rise beyond the ego and superconsciously
experience unifying exalted spirit. If this grand achievement
is attained while living, in our daily lives we are freed of the
wanting self and see the divine spirit in all.

When our self-fullness keeps us from any aspect of our
individual authentic spiritual journey, we are prevented from
progressing in our evolution to joining the perpetual unifying field of LoveSource—that is, our one being One. Our
self-fullness, obsessed as we are with filling ourselves with
what our lower mind wants, limits us and blinds us, and the
fullness we think we gain is false, emptied by time.

A true moment of selflessness is a taste of the Infinite. We
are released from the prison of self. Remaining in the prison of
the wanting self, we can never achieve true lasting happiness
and contentment. The high of a win—a gambling payout, a

promotion, a shiny new car—dissipates. An elevation into selflessness, however momentary or lasting, is beingness on a higher plane. When we are earthbound, that higher plane is invisible, seemingly impossible to detect with all the strife in the world and in our mind. But it is there. We don't need better self-aggrandizement. Rather, we need a Master who has the key to unlock us from our prison.

A letting-go of ego, in meditation or selfless service, frees us of the separate self. This is an experience of relief. Relief from the worrisome self, the incomplete self that is all too aware of dissatisfaction. The more you experience selflessness, the more you enjoy the beatitudes of being. Our essence is love. Our true selves are emanations of divine Love. But to function on Earth, we have taken a body and a mind that dominates and obscures our soul. We will never find true contentment until we begin with humility to seek our reunion with the Source that is radiating within each of us, ultimately becoming liberating unifying selflessness.

37 Oneing Experiences Those Lustrous Moments

Sitting alone, gazing at the objects of your home, appreciating the play of light on a plant, a chair, a lamp, a favorite purchase, taking in the whole room where you are situated, you begin to lose yourself as you take in the fullness of the moments. This is an experience of oneing. You exist with the totality of everything around you and within you. You transcend your everyday thoughts and concerns and exist in timeless lustrous moments.

The skins that encompass the bodies of people, the shells of objects are but an illusion—false boundaries and barriers to perceiving God in everything. Your consciousness can rise above this material world and ultimately see that spirit pervades everything. The pain we feel is that of separation. It is the soul's longing for its true Home, God-realized Spirit.

Being quiet—even in a bustling crowd—being still, taking in the movement and ongoingness of life, you can let go and loosen your indivi*duality* and feel at one. The persistent ploy of the mind is to keep you feeling separate, searching for that which would fill you with its wants. But you have everything you need right now. It's just taking the opportunity to take time out, relax, and leave your thoughts behind as you experience your oneness.

Feel gratitude as you appreciate the luster when you look and see. Relax, breathe, enjoy…. Peace will feel at home within you. You will know when to move on. You also may know what to attend to, how to handle a situation. Issues that were unclear before may now be clear.

Return to oneing as your private refuge, as your carefree meditation in which you let go (and there's no question of how "well" you do). You can simply be and appreciate the lustrous divine, which is keen for your remembrance. For if you let go of yourself and feel the elusive infinite self, you can absorb that luster.

The busyness imposed on us from without and within is just the job of the mind—yours and those you take in—to keep you caught up in time, experiencing everything your mind insists on, time after time. A little rebellion, a little time-out, is a good thing. Be aware of the One during lunch, for instance, to stop chewing, watching, or reading, and look. Breathe and sigh and see the beauty around you. Allow the Presence to emerge and create those lustrous moments that truly will feed your soul.

38 Mythical Misperceptions

"Time doesn't stop." Authors have written this in various contexts. The lives of many are run by the urgency of time, enslaved by self-imposed and/or externally imposed deadlines to get everything done. Others are driven to fulfill desire after desire, perhaps believing that this is the best way to fill up the time of their days. And some simply want to lose themselves to eat, drink, and be merry in media, oblivious that their time is running out. Unlike in a game of sports, you can't run out the clock to win. The only way your clock will run out this lifetime is when you die. But does it really? Until you transcend the realities of time by attaining a higher transcendent conscious reality, you will be subject to time in different births and destinies. Regardless, time passing is the condition that binds our lives.

The strictures of time are a constant looming over our lives. Before we are born, an automatic loom weaves the fabric of our lives with the threads of destiny for this life. When you are born, your "baby blanket" has been woven into the fabric of your life—your destiny. But some may experience timeless moments when their awareness is suspended in a higher place. They lose their individual sense of self and seem to exist on a freer plane.

This could occur in a creative act when, with full ongoing concentration, you seem to merge in your art when painting, playing music, realizing a poem, and it's a transcendent experience—there's just the act of making art. Time has fallen away.

Another experience of timelessness can be a seeing a beloved after a long absence when you gaze into each other's eyes and lose all sense of yourself—time seems to stop. Still another could be during meditation when, with full, ongoing concentration you let go, transcend thought, and your consciousness soars in a timeless beatitude. The ticking of thoughts, like the ticking of an old clock, has wound down and stopped. That is, until your thought machine insistently returns.

The tough rub is that during these seemingly timeless experiences of being, time is running. What if these sublime tastes of creation, of love, of meditation are hints of a higher reality in which time does not merely seem to stop? Time is *gone.* You exist beyond time and space in an exalted state of being, truly awakened and your realer self.

Time is a myth. It is an abiding myth in this planetary prison in which we are serving our term for a particular time—a preordained number of days and breaths. When we die, we will exist in an altered state of time—be it sub-astral, astral, or causal until that time is up and we return to a planet to be in the physical for another preordained time. So here and elsewhere time does not stop. *But it can.*

In meditation, when you pass through an energetic aperture and your consciousness ascends, realizing subtler, finer energetic planes (the astral and then the causal) with a fully realized Guide, you can focus on your spiritual practice, traverse those regions and, with grace, pay off all your karmas and then disassociate from the mind and enter the first purely spiritual region. That is how you realize the end of time. What can be more inspiring and ennobling to know that you can be released from the prison of time and space and achieve real independence?

"Life, Liberty and the pursuit of Happiness." That phrase, that promise has inspired and empowered aspirants around the world for generations. "We hold these truths to be self-evident that all men are created equal, that they are endowed by their Creator with certain unalienable Rights, that among these are Life, Liberty and the pursuit of Happiness." This is the second sentence of "The unanimous Declaration of the thirteen united States of America."

The United States Declaration of Independence is a soul-shining, mind-inspiring promise, ideal, and powerful incentive. Many nations have adopted this or similar wording into their constitutions. This declaration of a divine covenant has empowered people to strive for the best goodness their life on Earth can deliver that they believe is *possible*. But while this promise is motivating, the belief that this can be obtained as a reality is a myth.

Something that is real *is lasting*. This life must end. During this life, we are saddled with a mad, ruling mind, riffing off a welter of desires and thoughts that prevent us from attaining true, lasting happiness. For most, the pursuit of happiness keeps us committing actions that accumulate ever more karmic debts and constrain us from achieving true liberty because these debts along with karmas from past lifetimes will form the destinies of future lives. These future lives, which are to be parceled out from each mind and soul's vast reserve of karmas, by definition eliminate liberty. They keep you coming back to live through yet another destiny of hope and heartbreak.

True liberty is that which you attain when all of your karmic debts are paid off and you are free to release the mind, which merges into universal mind, its natural home. Leaving your mind behind, you exist as soul and realize the first wholly spiritual realm. You attain self-realization—you know that the true you is soul and have direct perception that is beyond the confines of time and space. If you experience this while occupying a physical body, when you come out of your meditation, you will return to your space-and-time activities of eating, eliminating, thinking and doing, sleeping, aging. Time will not pass fast enough until you can meditate again to re-embark on that inner journey with your Guide. Such soul-fulfilling rapture! You have advanced toward gaining your true Home.

"Home Sweet Home." That saying of comfort adorns plaques and signs on walls of homes in English and other languages. "Home, sweet home" is also what many of us repeat when we return from a trip or a difficult day at work. More critically, the saying or its equivalent, however we imagine it, is a lodestar for many. For example, we might hope for a family to fill a home in the future, the home of our original nuclear family (when we're apart from it), or an imagined ideal family in a sweet home we fantasize about when the situation we are stuck in offers no other relief.

Homes and families have broken up because warring egos left no other alternative. Or for those forced to remain, their homes are staging grounds of abuse with ongoing threats and acts of physical and/or sexual violence; or a battlefield of verbal and emotional overt and covert warfare; or caretaker neglect of basic needs, stymieing the potential benevolent growth and maturation of children.

Millions of people throughout the world do not have homes. Or they subsist in flimsy structures of cardboard, cloth, plastic. Or their homes are infused with toxic elements like poisoned water or noxious fumes. Or they had sweet homes that seemed always secure but were destroyed by war or natural disasters. What is secure on this physical plane?

Life-changing events happen every day throughout the world, giving rise to millions of runaways, refugees, and evacuees seeking a safe, sweet home. And their only welcome? It could be a cold street, starvation, slavery, death.

"There's no place like home." That saying is in perhaps the most beloved iconic movie of the modern era: *The Wizard of Oz*. That's what Dorothy repeats in the land of Oz to return home to Aunt Em and Uncle Henry. "There is no place like home" is what Dorothy tells the scarecrow in the original book not long after a cyclone raised and carried her and her dog Toto in their home up and away from Kansas and landed them in the land of Oz. She has set out to ask the Wizard of Oz to return her home. The longing and love to return home is what motivates her to brave dangers and challenges, and Glinda the Good Witch reveals the "wonderful powers" Dorothy has to return home.

The longing for home is a potent force. Regardless of how humble a home we occupy at this time, the sweetly, painful longing for our true Home is always present. Even when we're not aware of it. That is the longing of the soul to return to its original abode. The paragon of having and keeping a sweet home on Earth is a myth. Certainly, there are those whose current destinies have blessed them with a sweet home for the years and days until it is no longer. But the misconception that there is or can be or should be no place like home is a myth that keeps us blinded from seeking, discovering, and experiencing the spiritual journey to our true Home, the eternal abode that is imperishable.

Who we are is soul, presently occupying a body with a mind, a slave to the senses that have dominated us for eons. Our soul is our true being of consciousness, free of mind and body, whose one constant longing is to return to our true Home, an infinite sweet surging sea of pure, eternal love. That's not a mythical misconception. It is our heritage.

39 A Saint Comes Calling

Imagine for a moment that you've been going through a period of isolation. You've been diligently attending to your work, hardly speaking to a soul, doing your best to keep your emotions together. In your own way, you've been trying to live a good life. Then one day, in the middle of the afternoon, a Saint comes calling.

After you open your door, for an endless moment, your mind is somewhere else. Finally, you gather your senses and invite them in. They sit across from you at your table. This Saint could be anyone you would most like to see. Living, or passed on and come back just for you: St. Theresa of Ávila; Mary, mother of Jesus Christ; Gautama Buddha; St. John of the Cross; Rumi; Soami Ji of Agra; Guru Nanak; a great Master; even Jesus Christ.

As they sit across from you, their eyes are an unfathomable ocean of light and love; they look into your eyes; you lose yourself, soaring in an absorption of bliss.

They speak, bringing you back, asking you questions. You talk about your life. You are feeling comfortable, perfectly at home, when they ask, "What's been weighing on your mind?"

You open your heart and share your deepest concerns and questions. In this precious interchange, you know they know you better than yourself. You are filled with your Saint. Before you are ready—yet you're filled with love—they rise and say they will return in a week.

That evening, you can't stop thinking: *the Saint is coming calling.* You wonder what to do. Immediately you know—clean your place. You clean every surface, even inside the cabinets and under the tabletop. Each day, you sweep the entrance.

Several nights later, while you are brushing your teeth, it hits you—what about your thoughts? You want your thoughts to be clean. Positive. Good. Loving. Self-effacing. You clean your place again the day before the anticipated arrival, feeling love with each wipe of the rag, now finding spots that escaped your attention before.

A week later to the minute, again the Saint comes calling. Your smile seems to stretch across your face. You try to absorb every sight of their face and word of the visit. After an unknown time of gazing into those lustrous eyes, you thank them again and again for coming and ask if you may ask a question. "Please, please, my pleasure," is the response. You ask, "Can you tell me my purpose?" With an elegant splay of their fingers, they say, "To find God."

You try to ponder it, but your mind is somewhere else. The Saint's presence is so huge, it seems to infuse every molecule of your place and radiate for miles. Before you're ready, they rise, thank you sweetly for the visit, and they have left you with their Presence.

For the next week, you are not your usual self. Spontaneous grins open your countenance; hope washes over you; your legs feel like air and your head seems to contain heavens.

As days pass, you try to recall things they said, but it's as if the words have evaporated. You become frustrated and wonder if it was real, but you felt more alive than ever and a love that was beyond words. Then you feel something on the edge of your mind. What was it? You go about your day and then it comes to you, a strange word: talisman. They left you with a talisman. At your front door, just before they left, they looked at you with light-dancing eyes and said, "You can find me within."

Your being thrills. You're not clear what it means. Ah, but the prospect! Suddenly, it feels as though your whole life has shifted. A path that was obscure you now know lies close by. You just need to seek it. You don't know if the Saint will come again. You feel sadly, no. But feel with a marvelous certainty that you are ready to start discovering.

40 Guess Questions

Sometimes or oft times you don't know what to do. You either are faced with an overabundance of options or don't know what to attend to in a given moment. Duties, tasks, and desires—in work, relationships, health, home, recreation— can jostle your thinking with competing priorities and even commanding exigencies. Moreover, you may need to attend to a critical matter but presently you're not aware of it, or you may only feel that phantom lurking somewhere in your mind.

Learning to know how to live your best, most worth- while life is figuring out what to do next and soon and later. An invaluable means to mastering this is to guess questions. Asking yourself the right questions with the best focus, word- ing, and sequencing is as essential as knowing whether the answers you get are true or not.

Guessing the right questions is a key to facilitating and advancing self-realization. You can experience inner assur- ance, growth, stalwartness, and evolution by making this process your companion. By becoming sophisticated in its execution, you open a treasure of possibilities and guessing questions mines them. These possibilities await you, and becoming proficient at asking the right questions is a matter of interest, devotion, practice, learning, refinement, and knowing what you get is true and also what you can't know presently. At times, the answer will need to filter through your consciousness all day (and night) and then when you're preparing to go to bed or the next morning, it may come through to your awareness—and you just know.

Guess and ask questions when you're stuck and pulled in several directions or no direction. If you're busy and you feel it's not the optimal time, you can wait until you feel free and relaxed. Another situation is when having nothing to do lurches about as a monster in your head, making you anxious, and then you realize you want to hunt it down to vanquish it and finally know what will occupy and satisfy your mind.

You can sit comfortably and gaze at a view, or you may feel pulled to lie on the floor or a yoga mat and breathe easily, letting any kinks unkink. You can address your higher knowing mentally (or verbally) in any way you wish, for instance, *Dear Higher Self; Say, Susan; Listen, Frank; Dear God*. Then mentally address that willing, helpful awareness with which you feel a connection. *Dear God, I wish to know what next to do that will serve and support my better self and instill contentment. Is this something I can know now?* If you get a "yes," if you feel *yes*, the field of guessing questions is open. Guess which questions to ask, and feel good about asking, using the process you have learned, practiced, and come to have faith in, especially your connection to that higher knowing.

As you explore and refine your process, you can think of it as a treasure hunt, a blessed chocolate Easter egg hunt, to further awakening and knowing how to keep realizing your best life and self. You don't need to feel or believe that you are on your own or that this is beyond your native abilities because you *do possess* higher connectivity within your consciousness. This is your gift as a human being.

41 The Dangerous Balm of Forgetfulness

I forget things all the time. Especially what people tell me. I make a great confidant. Is it because my mind is so busy, or that I am totally present in the moment, comprehending their communication? In either case, any remembrance of our engaging interchange is lost.

My fellow mortals also forget all kinds of things: keys, remotes, birthdays, friends, resolutions, appointments, death at our doorstep. The mind's wayward willfulness secretes and attaches to thought after thought, desire after desire, forgetting, indulging in the balm of forgetfulness. Like a child walking home from school repeating, "Step on a crack, you'll break your mother's back," skipping over cracks in the pavement but sometimes landing on a crack accidentally (on purpose), then jumping with both feet into a puddle of mud, our mind loves to play with sensations, images, little monstrous daydreams. This works well to distract us from and assuage the pains and misunderstood troubles of life.

This salving with balms, these mental escapes keep the bad willies at bay, yet continue to coat the soul with mud.

Regardless of the qualities of your mind—quick or slow to express thoughts, observant or obtuse, daydreamy or delirious with ambition—it is doing a bang-up job, having battered your soul and battened down its innate inclination to be free and again be merged with God.

Your free will was squandered untold lives ago as your mind took control and lost itself in the physical senses and the desires that took over, racking up and stockpiling karmas to be divvied out in your destinies to come.

Now, here you are, on Earth. Not an easy planet to dwell on, as planets go. It is the school of hard knocks; that is, if you pay attention and make good use of your time here, you can evolve, awaken further. Each of us has a well-stocked medicine chest of balms. Each balm is designated to distract, to soothe or excite, and to make us forget whatever has been hard, hurtful, unpleasant, or nagging at us that day or from days long ago. Whether it is a killer reality show, a romance novel, drinks with friends, or a heavenly glazed donut, they each serve to make us forget. We forget what's troubling us, for a time that ends too soon. No matter how traumatic or blah our state of mind, our self-prescribed balms medicate and serve a purpose, especially when they rebalance our mind in a good way.

If you are aware of them and acknowledge them for the purpose they fulfill, you can observe your engagement with a certain detachment, even rising above this dependency to an extent. And then enjoy your enjoyment of them. But how aware are we of the ongoing dangerous balm of forgetfulness? As helpful as many of our balms may be to rebalance our mind and get us through the day, by bathing in the forgetfulness they induce, they make us forget that death is always at our doorstep and that we are missing the rare and precious opportunity of this life.

The worldly balms of forgetfulness further enshroud our spiritual apprehension and separate us from God. The invisible weight we carry also represents a mountain of missed opportunities that keeps swelling, lurching higher, as we pursue our passions heedlessly, accruing the karmic debts that must be paid. We have been allotted our human life not only because of the debts that have finally become due, but because this is our chance to realize God. The fundamental truth is that when we are lost in the creation, we forget the Creator.

This is our precious opportunity to imbibe the tincture of remembrance and, by remembering God, we begin to transmute into becoming who we truly are. Long, long, long ago, we began to forget the real celestial balm in which we reveled. This was and is our original country, our true Home of pure complete consciousness. That is way beyond our individual grasping mind. What is further dangerous is that we are unaware of where our mind's induced actions have taken us and what lies in store for us. What horribly hurtful actions did we commit in our past lives? But the ever-looming karmas that are waiting to be played out and paid off can be forgiven and eliminated by following a true path of remembrance. Once we find and follow this path of remembrance, we can slowly and naturally rise above our sundry transient balms, and, with our inner Guide, travel within to gain the eternal, ever-renewing elixir—the divine Ocean of unalloyed fulfillment and perfect contentment.

42 Awe

Being taken up while your everyday cares are somewhere else, your higher self soars in grace, peace, and love.

When the seeker is ripe, hungering for God, struggling with all life has scheduled, yet still being a good person, humbly not expecting, the receptivity may allow an inner upliftment, an experience of bliss, of grace.

This is also what it can be like (and *much more*) when you come into the presence of a perfect person. Gazing at them, waves of love may wash over you and you sail in a rarefied sky of grace and mercy. The soul exults in joy, for in this perfect person, peace, serenity, and love reign supreme. The soul rises in joy in this instantaneous recognition of itself fully realized, yet brilliantly alive in a human being. For eternal moments, the barrier between the temporal and the eternal is overcome.

Be wary of coming into the presence of a perfect person. Your whole life may change. Nothing else will come close. That is, if something is triggered within you. Awe.

Pure, unassuming devotion to God may inspire the awe within you. But also coming into contact with one who has realized God. The awe may bloom instantly, steadily over several days, or five years later if you carry the presence within you. Being in the presence of such a one is the ripest condition, for your soul may recognize a kinship and know: this is the one who will free me.

Gazing at this perfect person who has fully realized their divine Self is an experience unlike any other. You are taken up, forgetting yourself, your mind left somewhere far away. Your attention is riveted and your eyes cannot absorb enough of that exalted being. If only your body was covered with all-seeing eyes, would that be enough? Who is this perfect person who can inspire such exaltation?

Call them a realized Master, a true Saint, an inner Guide. The terms name one and the same. Once you meet a fully realized Master, it is the beginning of the end. The sojourns on this planet and others will be completed. It may be two lifetimes from now, or eight, or this very lifetime. If you do not happen to find such a One, you can continue to seek and ask for the true path of liberation of the soul from all the humdrum agonies of living separated from the sheer love and awe-filled bliss that is awaiting your realization.

Depending on your receptivity, upon first meeting this perfect person (and this is confirmed and reconfirmed the more you enjoy contact and observe them), you will experience the most compelling riveting sight ever. Regardless of how congruently handsome their features are, no face holds such beauty and attraction. They are so wondrously alive that all other objects seem lifeless in comparison. If you meet them with wary disbelief, a show-me attitude, this may be automatically displaced by delighting in how wondrous and compelling this human is. You will feel awe. Or not. It depends on your receptivity, your spiritualization at this point in your journey, and the will of God.

The other disbelief you may experience is that such a being exists. Even so, your higher knowing may apprehend that you have met a complete human—in other words, one who has fulfilled their inherent potential to realize God.

What is the perfect person like as you observe this one talking, responding to questions, interacting with those around them? At some point, you realize there is a complete absence of ego. Their utterances do not run the gamut from autobiographical to critical. Rather, you feel as if each word bathes you in a benevolent balm. You notice there is no calculation. They are the embodiment of giving, always serving those in their community and outside their community, if there is a need. They demonstrate a complete generosity of spirit, unrivaled positivity, pure humility, and, you sense, all this resides with unlimited power. Can all this be present in one person? Yes.

To be in the physical presence of a true Master, you absorb their spirituality. Being in their presence supercharges the process of realizing yourself.

If you do not presently have the opportunity to find and visit a true living Saint, you can visualize one as best you can where you are, in the privacy of your bedroom or bathroom or chewing your food. Imagine eyes luminous with layers and layers of light, an ocean of limitless love into which you want to fall. This may inspire awe.

Have faith, take heart. Follow and own your spiritual path with inner confidence. You are one of God's own. Your soul is longing to be born in awe.

43 The Herald of Remembrance

Can you remember who you are, where you're from?

Human beings, unlike other sentient beings, possess this faculty. But it remains dormant, unawakened in our consciousness. Even highly spiritual persons need someone to enable them to transcend their current awareness to access the remembrance of which they have been deprived.

So engrossed are we in our current life that we remain unaware of the veils of forgetting wrapped securely around our consciousness. Even the most spiritual of us require a herald. This herald is no ordinary messenger who regales us with feel-much-better sermons. This is a Herald who embodies Truth and who comes to enlighten us about our present state and, critically, who we truly are.

This Herald can assuage your long-lurking inner longing and grieving to be back where you belong.

Pursuing your pleasures and desires has engrossed your mind. That can provide temporary relief and distraction. But all too soon, life's demands require you. Is it an easy matter to get through each hour of each day, to show up and perform at work, at home, and somehow also make time to take care of yourself? No wonder your actual identity and state of being were enshrouded and forgotten long, long ago.

To whatever degree we are aware of it, we suffer from being caught up in this particular life, estranged from our true Home. Most of us suffer unknowingly, having to live with a shifting, false identity, not realizing it is false. Being cast in this state of non-remembrance, we also suffer not knowing when we are going to die and what we are going to have to go through before we can die. But it is also having no idea what we will go through *after* you die. Worst of all, it is not knowing the precious opportunity you had while you were alive to begin to remember.

Heralds appear from time to time in different places, in different cultures, but they are not of that place or culture. These Heralds of remembrance are human beings—but much, much more. They are humans who have recovered their all-knowingness. Having surpassed mind and intellect in their consciousness, existing always on the highest of planes, they come on missions of mercy to those who are aching or simply ready to engage in the process of remembrance.

These exalted Heralds impart truths of the soul, our cosmos, and the finer, higher realms of being in the mode of the current culture in the way their initiates can readily grasp. Regardless of how fine or wanting you may deem your character and spirituality, if you are meant to regain your true divine Self, a Herald will ensure you will find them and guide you mystically in just the way that suits you.

First, through their teachings, the Herald imparts the secrets of life and death, the Supreme Being, and the creation. Then when you are ready, they initiate you into a practice of remembrance that gradually and surely dissolves the veils of false identities. This true meditation on the inner mystical Sound and Light (aka the Word, Shabd Dhun) is a slow and assured process of awakening to who you truly are.

We are all suffering in our individual ways from what we have to go through day after day. But we are also suffering from not knowing why we are here, now on our spot on Earth in these particular changing circumstances with those people in our life who come and leave.

Is this actually a creation of the Supreme Being, or is it the Big Bang playing itself out, devoid of a pervasive loving consciousness? If either, how did the universe come into being? Why do the denizens of Earth have such different circumstances and lives? Can any of it ever make sense? What really happens when you die? This existential pain gnaws at us even when we are not aware of it.

Believe it or not, we live in a benevolent universe. There is hope. Actually, there is more than hope. We have an opportunity—if we are so moved—for everything to make sense, to be relieved of our mental and soulful burden of this life and to finally understand—initially intellectually and ultimately via direct perception—all the whys and wherefores of existence and to enjoy *comfort*.

If you come into contact with a Herald and gain initiation into meditation, if you follow their instructions devotedly, comfort will suffuse your mind, your being, your life beyond what you dreamed possible. What relief! What joy for this life, for your life to make sense and have meaning!

Knowing what the Herald imparts, you can readily inculcate detachment from the outrages of this world. Further, the real blooming love within you will also bring compassion for all who are suffering. If you are led to a Herald and commit to and follow the path of remembrance, this is the key to realizing yourself. This is the path of self-realization, of dissolving the false notions and obstructing veils that smother your soul awareness.

Initially, the meditation is the practice of remembering and repeating the empowered words the Herald has given you that are infused with their spirituality. With this repetition and listening to the divine Sound (to which you have been attuned at initiation), this path of remembrance is your evolution to a higher state of being. You are becoming transmuted into the being of your origin. Until it is mastered, your rambunctious mind will ride you with a wild will of its own; however, you can take comfort in your inner conviction and knowing that you are returning to your original state of Wakefulness. Once attained, there is no need to remember because now you are the Being that preceded your immersion and adventure in time and illusion.

44 The Grace of Anointment

Grace, unfathomable grace. To long for it, to work for it, to guess and grok its bestowals. This is the exalted adventure of the seeker. Is grace an unmerited reward? Can you know it? That you even think about grace—now, that is grace.

When you sense a connection to God within, those unexpected private miracles of uplift must surely be grace. But also, what we label as misfortunes, each deserving of our compassion, can be grace if you advantage them to turn within to God. (And never blame God—thank your self of another lifetime for sowing the seeds of this opportunity.) Yes, cleaving to the Wonder within—regardless of how dimly perceived—grace may be more readily showered and will enable you to go through those difficult times more positively, more open to higher guidance.

With an orientation that is authentically, humbly spiritual, grace is what you can win when you pursue your path to God with devotion. Then you are happy to be as receptive as possible in your private sanctuary of awareness. That is turning within to worship however you can. It is not beseeching God for miracles, for outcomes of your choosing. Worship is not your ego insisting, bargaining for its wants. Worship is remembering your Higher Power that always knows best and accepting with humility how your life plays out. It is all according to divine will and purpose.

Perhaps the greatest grace that has been waiting for you before the advent of time and all along when you ventured out into the realms of time and maya is to receive the anointment. The anointment is when a living human who is a fully awakened instrument of God mystically attunes you to the Audible God Stream and forever reverses your trajectory through the creation.

This anointment is an inner connection for you to *evolve into*, rather than having a priest or clergyperson dab blessed oil on your forehead. The mystical anointment is perfected within your very being. Your Teacher, the divine incarnation, awakens your soul to the Audible God Stream (aka the Sound Current, the Word). The anointment makes all the difference in how you experience the world. It bestows a divine gift that no matter what horrific suffering you must endure, *everything* will ultimately be all right.

The fully realized Teachers and Saints have a saying: "Once sown the seed never goes waste." With your anointment, this initiation, comes the daily practice of meditation, which is concentrating your attention at the eye center—the gateway to within—to collect your mind and soul currents to listen more readily to or for the divine Sound. The better you collect your attention by means of repetition and withdraw your consciousness from the body, you also see the divine Light. Meditation of listening to the Audible God Stream is consecrating yourself by cultivating your anointment rather than letting it go to waste.

The more you give of your time, your life, the more the anointment grows in your consciousness. Your very being is being transmuted to the frequency of the Beloved. The Beloved is your Teacher-Guide who projects from the Sound Current into the subtle astral form of their physical form within your consciousness. This way, once you have withdrawn enough in the inner journey, you recognize them with your soul's power of seeing in their brilliantly illumined Radiant Form. By repeating the empowered names given to you at initiation, you can test their identity and are not led astray by imposters on your inner journey.

If you don't receive the anointment this lifetime, that is okay. You can be aware of it, remember it. You can seek a Saint, a fully realized Teacher-Guide, listen to their discourses and answers to questions and, being in their Presence, absorb the spiritually charged atmosphere. If you are irrepressibly pulled to seek and receive that inner anointment, that is the supreme grace for us mortals. It marks the beginning of the end of your wandering through life after life with your mistaken identity—mind and ego—committing actions whose seeds will bear sweet or bitter fruit.

However your destiny unfolds in this lifetime, if you receive the anointment, you are enfolded in the loving, protective embrace of your God-realized Guide who initiated you. This is a gift that your gratitude can reciprocate each day by being your best in meditation and empowering and expressing the good qualities of a human being.

If you cherish an attachment to a divine personage who has left this plane of mortality, ask yourself: Is God's grace limited? Can the vessel of a living human form be filled but once? Will your ardent belief in that glorious historical figure be enough to reunite you with God? Adhering to a Savior or Guru who is long gone is the sly winning strategy of the mind that deprives you of meeting and believing in a living vessel of God. Rather, you adhere to outer rites and rituals and are deprived of the opportunity (for which you were born) of seeking anointment to journey Home finally via the eternal Audible Life Stream while still living and beyond. Only when you receive the anointment from a realized living Guide can you meditate on the divine Light and Sound.

While you and a Guide are in the flesh, this anointment is your possibility, your potential for realizing yourself, the true Self, as a spark of the Eternal Consciousness. Allow yourself to meditate on the supreme gift of grace that is available to us all.

45 Your Ether Wings

Did you learn to swim using water wings? Water wings are inflatable plastic cylindrical bands worn on the upper arms. The air inside the bands helps keep the swimmer afloat. Thus, the beginning swimmer can try the front crawl, learning how to swim with much less concern for going under.

We are alone. From the moment we come into this world until we are taken out of it. We must learn to navigate all the challenges of living. Initially, we may get help from parents, caretakers, and teachers. But when you are an adult, even with a wise and caring partner or devoted best friend, you must chart and travel your own trajectory each moment, venture, alternative. Friends and therapists may provide opinions, but they don't know the whole you and not necessarily what is best for you.

Self-reliance is all very good, but what if that self is unsure, unduly influenced, or under the sway of the ego and other negative passions? Wouldn't it be wonderful to have an all-knowing friend within you? That is, within your awareness. A higher knowing, a guide you could turn to whenever you were leery of getting into a situation or you were thrashing about getting nowhere. You have the capacity and the potential to access an inner guide, a higher consciousness. The first step is to nurture the keen desire to have an inner guide.

Your keen desire must embrace a belief that your awareness can access a higher consciousness you can develop and work with. Further, you must commit to a willingness to experiment with how this inner guidance develops. You can learn to know it and allow it and perhaps it will help if you understand what makes you human.

You possess the *active* primordial element of ether. This is not a chemical element but one of the five creative energies or essences—the primal divine emanations—that are the warp and woof of created mental and physical existential planes of relative realities. Ether, or *akasha* in Sanskrit, could also be called the substance of all space. Akasha is the hidden energy from which the universe originates.

What is critical to appreciate is that *presently* you are the winner of the existential lottery: possessing ether in its active state, humans have the capacity to distinguish between right and wrong, commit right and wrong actions, knowingly worship God or go away from God, and achieve God-realization. We can be aware that we live as physical human beings and that we will die. When thrown into the raging river that rushes us to death, we can sink or swim.

We can prepare for our impending death. The better our comprehension of reality—the ongoing play of continually unfolding life, the soul's journey back to God—the better we can know how we can make best use of our life. Hence, we can find our inner guide, learn to live a proficiently worthwhile existence, and ultimately reap our spiritual fortune. Because we are connected to divinity (regardless of our level of awareness), we can learn how to swim toward that welcoming sea of knowing, love, and soul delight.

Briefly, this is the concept of your ether wings' inner guide. What about your guide as a companion? First, realize that this interaction and communication are going to happen in your awareness, which will become increasingly cognizant with practice and discovery. Second, realize that you are aiming to focus on your higher mind, the mind that can be friend to your soul. The mind—the lower mind—can be a trickster, a hooligan, a usurper of our attention. But you have intuition, will, and most important, the Supreme Being is more willing than you can fathom for you to realize your inner connection.

If you believe or once believed in Jesus, in Krishna, in Buddha, or any exalted Master, why not accept that, with practice and grace, your consciousness can gain the higher heavens while you are still alive? But also, if you feel an inner pull, that you can seek a realized *living* Master whose perfected all-knowingness can guide you all the way Home? With initiation and the explicit instructions of meditation, you can gain this inner Guide, who is with you and within you all the time. This will give your ether wings added buoyancy and true guidance to swim meditatively through life and happily pass through death to your loving, waiting Guide.

If you don't feel an inner pull to seek a living inner Guide, that's fine. It is not in your destiny this time around. Regardless, you possess that inner etheric connection, and God's grace and love are perfectly companionable. With your attention collected (more and more) at your eye center—the seat of your soul between and behind your eyes—you can feel the Presence. You can nurture and cherish the Presence—a loving companionship, a benevolent guidance. You can think of it as as divine or, if this does not resonate with you, ethereal, heavenly, auspicious, or simply benevolent.

No matter how tough your life is or how much you screw up, you can turn within, let go and know this past is behind you, and suss out your next step. That might be being still, then enjoying a marvelous stretch, and then you may just know! With whatever inner guidance you sense, be and do your best. Swat away negative thoughts that keep surfacing in your awareness. All those hurts, those cutting rejections, and assumed failures are only the mind's repeated negative expressions. Don't let them disturb your peace and take you away from your spiritual center. You are finding your way into a new country of being. Be kind to yourself and practice the language of this new relationship. It may seem foreign, but it is your birthright. Eventually, you will live a vital, sustaining inner life that grants peace and helps you rise above conflicting currents to find your authentic way.

Your efforts to find your authentic way illuminate an auspicious truth of engaging with your ether wings' inner guide. That is, you are utilizing your inherent powers, doing your best, to align with the Will. You are developing and transforming your God-given life to live in harmony with divinity. Thus, each time you turn within for contact and guidance, it is an effort to mold your thoughts and actions to please God. That is manifesting grace. With effort and grace, effort and grace, that beneficent inner dance, you are finding your way to be with God. Your akasha is transforming into that higher, creative love. This is something to celebrate and give thanks for with inner gratitude.

46 Sparks of Being Complete

In a reflective moment, a moment when you're not aware of being you, you may notice a spark. This spark means you are complete. It can also mean that what you have been attending to is complete. It is a feeling, a knowing that everything is all right. Better than all right. You are whole and also it can come through that you are a whole part of the Whole.

At times during your day and throughout your life, you may experience the spark of being complete. Here's a mundane example. You're dishing out cereal and you want just the right amount. You shake out or finger out pieces until you feel it's just the right amount in your bowl. Or perhaps a feeling comes through—it's a bit much. You take pieces away, putting them back in the cereal bag until it registers that you know it's the right amount. When you are consciously attending, the same thing can be experienced when you pour in the milk.

Another example is when you are writing an email or a letter with a number of issues and fine points to express. You write it out. You go back over it, correcting typos, writing details and points you'd earlier thought of and are now remembering. If you are responding to a correspondence, you go back over that sentence by sentence, registering whether you have fully addressed all of their concerns and expressed your point of view. With this in mind, feeling good about being diligent, you review your correspondence, adding and deleting words, phrases, sentences, making your communication more concise and complete. If the communication is very important, you may wait a few hours or a day and then go back over it again, revising, proofreading, and spellchecking until you experience that feeling—a spark of knowing conveys that the correspondence is complete. You send it, feeling good.

A third example you may have experienced is a conversation with a soul friend. A soul friend is a kindred spirit with whom you can share what you need to communicate without concern of judgment or censure. This is a friend who knows you well, who knows what is presently pertinent about your history and struggles, your highs and lows. It may have been weeks, months, or longer since you conversed and much has happened or may happen that you wish to share. At the right time on the phone, a video call, or in person, your voices and kind intentions meet and you exchange your news and possibilities, disquiets and support. It feels good to be engaged and communing with your soul friend. You want the best for them. At a certain point when it feels that everything that's been needed to be shared has been, you may sense a spark— this is complete. You say, "Goodbye, *much love*," feeling good, whole.

In this meditation, complete can convey one or more of these meanings: brought to an end or to a final or intended condition; fully realized; possessing all that is necessary. Spark can mean a realization of knowing that you are or something is complete. This may come through as an unarticulated knowing, a feeling, an understanding, or as a conscious registering and acknowledging. The after-sense of the spark may linger; it can be a wonderfully full inner glow that stays with you and, in time, dissipates. Or it can be quickly snuffed out by your thoughts or events.

Spark also has a more profound, mystical meaning. The word spark represents a living, eternal particle, a vestige of pure spirit that is of the divine. The spark is you. Complete in its unrealized state. It is also pure potential. Perfect pure potential that can realize its divinity. That is because, as humans, each of us has the potential to clear our karmic accounts, complete our sojourns in life form after life form, purify and intensify the brilliance of our spark to that of many, many suns, ultimately to rejoin the eternal Origin.

You are a microcosm that contains the macrocosm. The macrocosm is universes within greater, higher universes, all with their relative realities, vibrational levels, and admixtures of matter, mind, and spirit. God, the creation, *is within us*, for we, our souls, are each sparks of God. Our spark of being can concentrate and collect its attention at the eye center to rise to the third eye (*if therefore thine eye be single*) and withdraw through the aperture within each of us to enter the beginning of multiverses that exist successively at finer, higher, more subtle frequencies. Here, in the physical, you possess the entry to the beginning of the macrocosm.

The six chakras or energetic centers within our physical

bodies are reflections of six chakras of the next higher realms which, in turn, are reflections of six higher centers, each powering multiverses that dwarf our physical universe and cannot be fathomed, only barely imagined. As you rise and progress within, you begin to sense infinities of sparks of more refined mind and realized spirit. The fully realized spirit that is infinitely complete is the Supreme Being.

That omnipotent Source is manifested through the multiverses of its Being. It exists everywhere, in every form, animate and inert, and here is the spark to really get: only as a human does it incarnate and is it able to realize its divinity. Thus, to realize our divinity, we need a complete Master. Complete in this context means a human being whose soul has risen beyond the mental realms and realized its Godhood while living in the physical. He or she knows the entire way of return and can ascend within at will *and* can guide their initiates—their yet-to-be fully realized sparks—on their journey of spiritual evolution to rejoin the Being that is Complete, that knows all and is all. We are blessed with the grace to possess the potential to know who we are and what we can become. The consummating sparks of becoming Complete is the ultimate, soul-enrapturing journey of realization.

47 Things Fall Away

At the tender age of seventy-two, I am aware of some of what has fallen away—friends, judgments, the need for socializing, the need to see and take in outer sights and experiences. Whether it has been the pandemic, aging, health challenges, refinement of energy, and greater absorption in my moment-to-moment spiritual path, the evolution to contentment is conspiring to shear away people and places, leaving a solitude in which I can revel in the spiritual Presence available to all of us.

When things fall away, what is the result? Freedom. Enhanced appreciation and love of my life. Grateful thanks go to the stealthy bliss that has been accumulating over decades of meditation and the practice of the Presence of God. In the Presence, or seeking it, I am gratefully, wonderfully content.

The falling away of things likely has much to do with the fact that before long I'll be leaving. Whether I will be relieved of the physical within eleven months or eleven years or beyond that, the years pass by more quickly because I'm living in the now, but ironically because I am doing very little out in the world.

Many years ago, when I saw particularly gorgeous people

and abandoned myself to stealing glances at their arresting faces and forms and later visualized them, seeking to inject myself into a phantom reality in which I would lose myself in that beauty—that was the ingrained tendency of my mind, which wanted to go out and out again, seeking and seeing better enthralling images. But they are transitory. Lifeless. A false hero's labyrinth peopled with false gods and goddesses who readily disappear or disappoint. The mystical boon is that when others fade or fall away, you can lose yourself in the One if you are receptive to the grace.

It's a relief to be coming to the end of this lifetime and becoming more keenly focused on readying my conscious-ness for the grand departure. I have been given to feel that this is my final departure. Whether I will have to take births in the causal region is something I am not allowed to know yet.

I have usually done my best to balance and fulfill my social needs. For years before COVID-19, typically it was two social contacts plus a spiritual service or two each week: lunch with a friend each week, dinner and a movie with a friend three times a month, attending a spiritual service weekly or twice a week. Now, even as COVID-19 wanes, it is reading spiri-tual literature several times a day, seeing my Teacher's Q & A online, and perhaps every two months sharing a restaurant lunch or dinner with one of the two friends who have not fallen away. That's it. And I am content.

I have become something of a hermit. It is a relief to have my outer and inner life so free and aligned that this embod-ied soul can be filled readily with inner joy. Yes, and with engagement, creativity, and the balancing balm of variety. In my solitary life with all this fullness, contentment blooms and blooms. The variety is my strategy and natural inclination for working with my mind and emotions to maintain and nurture my daily balance. Thus, in addition to meditation and writing, I read, walk and swim with my dog, work out, and take an evening break to watch the highest quality shows. It is important to *know* your mind and spirit, continuing to discover what works best, what supports equilibrium and contentment. Each morning, I intuit a particular spiritual focus for the day. Many mornings, I summon a special emphasis in my meditation to keep awakening inspiration and zeal.

To keep my mind happy with its need of variety for the physical, I choose colors of T-shirts and polos (usually varied shades of blues and greens) that feel best. Exercising my intuition, choice of food is creative, an appealing attunement to my nutritional needs and a particular combination of food—especially for lunch when I often make a smoothie with different milks, meal replacement powders, supplements, superfoods, fruits, and greens. It's a way of feeling complete. Satisfying a need. Being in sync with what's best now. Once these two intuitively curated experiences are complete, I feel good. That's contentment.

The contentment dividend grows, is reinvested with each passing day. The contentment dividend is enriched with immersion in cultivating the presence of God. Cultivating the presence of God is the true, all-weather balm that soothes contentment into the crevices of my mind. That Presence is the true reality that becomes realer the more things fall away. Our minds are so lost in outer things that perceptive discrimination is challenging. But we each have innate *vivek* (Sanskrit: discrimination).

With the practice of vivek, you can learn to access and enhance inner guidance. Ah, inner guidance. I remember well how much in my forties I desired it, craved it, felt I needed it. I was trying to figure out three major areas of my life: where to live, finding and nurturing a primary relationship, and what to write to fulfill and further me on my path of writing.

Writing! Rather than books and short works, actually, I have spent an inordinate amount of time writing query letters, book proposals, bios, media kits, and many other writing-*related* activities trying to launch my career so I could focus on writing books. Have I allowed anything else to create more frustration in my mind? No.

Not trying to find a partner. Not trying to be celibate. Not going back and forth between trying to find a love relationship and marriage (including with three women) and trying to be celibate and transcend that natural human need. Not for years trying to bury being gay because my path's organization did not accept its gay and lesbian initiates being sexually active. Not my inability to heal my acute, disabling back pain. Not being able to heal my adrenal and glandular exhaustion that kept life and clarity at bay. Going back years to a crucible of karma, my nuclear family: not my emotionally entwining, controlling, self-aggrandizing, guilting, dear, fantastic mother. Not my constantly verbally abusive and violent paranoid-schizophrenic brother whose acute hatred of me took sheer delight in punching me harder and harder and finding new ways to hurt and torment me. Not my ghost-monster of a father, who after orally raping me from the age of three through five abandoned me, never to engage in any fatherly interaction, be it conversation or teaching me how to throw and catch a ball. Not my so-believed to be good and faithful friends who I readily allowed to take advantage of me and betray me and impugn me when my efforts to mold myself to their liking did not measure up.

No, to use a cliché: writing takes the cake.

But all these frustrations eventually fell away thanks to meditation, cultivating my higher sense of knowing and accessing inner guidance, releasing self-damaging subconscious beliefs, appreciating the inherent goodness and helplessness of people, and growing wisdom and equilibrium.

As people enter their final years, many get desperate to do as much as they can out in the world. To what extent has their inner world been explored, healed, discovered, and evolved? Whatever is so is fine. Each of us has our own individual path. For many, what nags and diminishes their limited experience of happiness when going out in the world is their fear of death. Many are caught in clinging to this and to unresolved frustrations.

Some know the golden lining of getting older as physical death comes closer: things fall away and don't matter so much. What mattered so very much when I was younger has fallen away. Now it is about awakening further. During those previous ongoing mental tortures if my present older self could have met that younger self, I would have told him: "Do not indulge guilt, anxiety, worry. Be positive. Find and live the truth—what's true *now* within you of who you actually are and what is possible and what is practical. *Sense* and *weigh* how you will feel in thirty years. Ask yourself, 'Will I harbor regrets that I did not do such and such; that I did do something?' Remember, oft times we are ruled by our senses and passions. You will find yourself—even against your better judgment—going along on those rides. Allow yourself to believe and feel that it is all a learning experience. Also remember, recognize and value human connection, no matter how unlikely in place, time, and, most important, in person."

I would also tell him: "Let go of judgments of other people. Any negativity holds you back from the love and oneness you are seeking. All of these seemingly mean and poor-acting people are playing their part and will pass from your life. That is the unacknowledged salve of time. Judging binds you to them. Let things fall away, for this frees you to rise higher in awareness. With the tensions of mental ropes that keep pulling and tugging in your mind, how will they ever fall away? Whenever you are aware that you are judging someone or something, let go of it.

"Everything is unfolding in perfection, though almost everything *appears* to be grievously not right. People are ruled by their minds. They are usually trying their best, pulled this way and that by their self-controlling attachments. When they go out of their way to be mean, it is binding them further as slaves of their lower dark mind. Let these negative things fall away and allow yourself to feel content.

"Go through life and let go. Value, nurture, and embolden the Spirit within. Acknowledge and embrace that you are treading a path of enlightenment. The better you allow things to fall away, the better you will be filled with Light."

48 Goodbye to All That

I'll be leaving this Earth in—ten years, two years, fourteen and a half years, thirteen months? Like most people, I'm kept in darkness on this. Still passing through a period of extreme, exceptional pain after my prostate laser ablation, two urinary tract infections, and perhaps other complications, I'm looking forward more to a new life without this physical body that has allowed me to experience a fascinating life and pay off *gobs* of karma.

This world (that is not ours) is a stage for us to enjoy and suffer the consequences of our past actions. The seeming egregious unfairness is that people cannot see, cannot know why they are going through what they must. Why their life unfolds the way it does. What karmic debts they are expunging. The sly, outrageously tricky scheme of life is that virtually all people cannot see their personal, unique karmic web and what has been allotted to them this time round in their current life.

The challenge and the grace is to look beyond the detritus of life and sense within to cultivate the true connection. God, it's elusive! We've made it so. But it's there. *And* many of us in religious and spiritual past lives sought and furthered our divine connection.

Was it necessary for the Supreme Creative Being to send us down through lesser and lesser fields of Spirit? We cannot know until we return. Considering everything I know, it appears I am not returning to Earth once I am taken from this body. This mind&soul, still knotted together, will advance through the inner realms of less and less matter, more mind, more spirit, and, leaving the mind behind at the top of the mental plane, finally becoming purer and purer, all spirit.

My greatest disappointments have been people. Despite at times enjoying a communion of communication with dear friends, I have apparently held a deeper and higher regard than almost all of the friends in my life. I have experienced so much unkindness, disregard, betrayal, and lack of integrity that it has steadily, surely detached me from people. Now I embrace that as grace. After all, it is attachment that brings us back. What matters is my relationship with my Guide, who will guide me on my inner, mystical journey of return. More and more, I anticipate our meeting within, for then, the main veil will have been removed and I will commence the ever more joyous journey of becoming pure love-consciousness.

49 The Contentment Dividend

Wise, enlightened investment will create life beyond your best, fondest imagination. Spiritual investing will have a profound impact on the quality of your life and spiritual evolution. Consider four critical beneficences of investment. If you allow these opportunities to go to waste and only invest in worldly dross, the loss will be lamentable.

The first beneficence to consider and practice being aware of is how you invest your attention. How you invest your attention makes all the difference in your positivity of mind, degree of contentment, and spiritual evolution. Even if your higher mind is predominant a majority of the time, your lower mind can generate thoughts and images that are disturbing, down-pulling, troublemaking, and degrading. When your higher mind and attention are foremost, your mental state and activity are positive, well-meaning, benevolent, spiritually inclined, and naturally humble.

Thus, how you invest and divest your attention has a profound impact on your mental state and experience of contentment. When a negative thought or memory assails you, you can discard it no matter how often it pops up and disturbs you.

Regard your mind as an eternally sustainable popcorn popper popping thoughts throughout the morning, noon, afternoon, evening, and night. Some thoughts are salty, others are stale, peppery, cheesy, or saturated with unhealthy grease. But if your mind could be stilled and concentrated to stop popping and go within to drink the truly purifying blissful nectar, it would enjoy the sweetest of pleasures.

If you engage in meditation that includes the repetition of empowered words, this is an opportunity to employ it and override distracting, constant thoughts. If not, you can be a good parent to your insistent, obstreperous lower mind. You can exercise your will by internally (or externally) saying a firm but kind "Drop it," being detached, and knowing that these are the ingrained patterns of your wayward mental apparatus.

In creating a spiritual mental home for yourself wherever you happen to be, you can inhabit a benevolent, wise-acting apparatus. You can also exercise your inherent wisdom by intuiting and realizing when you need to rebalance yourself to return to equilibrium. For instance, if you have been concentrating with extreme focus, give yourself a break when the time is ripe to doodle, enjoy a puzzle, stroke a pet, stretch, or go outdoors, allowing your gaze to alight on the beauty around you. Although you have been conditioned by much throughout your life, you can develop a mastery of your awareness. First by being aware of your present awareness and then directing it to best serve your spiritual self. Whatever you discern with your higher knowing and engage in will rebalance you and shore up and maintain your level of contentment.

Contentment is very much a function of attention and will. Realize that you have the ability and power to know throughout the day where your attention is best focused and to exercise your power to direct it and redirect it as it gets pulled away by unwelcome, unhelpful thoughts and by external forces, particularly if someone or something obtrusively commands your attention. In time, you will possess the presence of mind to direct your attention and know best how to respond.

As your awareness improves of how you are investing your attention, and your attention resides in enhanced positivity and gratitude, this suffuses your experience of living with contentment.

The second beneficence is food. If we are fortunate to get it, we are able to eat food. Food has a perceptible, imperceptible, and profound bearing on our state of mind, human nature, future suffering, and contentment. Think of food as an investment in your being. What you eat incurs a light or heavy karmic debt. You can invest in foods that yield dividends or debts. Health or illness. A slight or heavy burden for what has been killed on your behalf.

If you overeat, if you eat food that does not agree with your system, if you consume chemically laden, artificial, or toxic food, you will likely feel the short-term and/or long-term effects, even to the point of chronic disease. Ideally, if we have the good fortune of choice and freedom to purchase, plus an inner knowing of what our body needs, we can invest in the food that will be nutritious, support our health, and help us feel good.

A wise saying is, "As we eat so we become." To what degree have you invested in violence and suffering? Knowing that their stomach is a graveyard for animals, how content can someone be?

It is a sad but true reality that to exist in the physical we must kill to eat. The greater the level of consciousness, the greater the suffering of the killed. Ingesting that violence and suffering forestalls the perfectibility of our human nature and adds to the burden our soul and mind must carry life after life.

Your small self-serving mind is adept at rationalizing anything. Whatever you eat that once lived accumulates karma. And the karma accumulated as you invest plant-based food in your body can be paid off far more easily. We invest for the future and, savoring yourself and your increasing well-being, you can take responsibility for taking the lowest form of life, thus minimizing your accumulating karmic debts and creating the conditions for a more salubrious and content future.

The third beneficence to be aware of is how well you invest your time. Following are three awarenesses to explore that can further your spiritual unfoldment and evolution. First, especially when you are feeling a little curious, devote yourself to seeking the truth about humankind's immortal questions. This can include ruminating about them when you wake up or walk. You can also find books by or sourced in the teachings of realized Masters who embody the truth. While seeking these available truths, practice exercising your discernment and embracing the conviction that you can know the true answers, *experience* the truth, and ultimately become the Truth.

The second awareness is to invest time in consciously and deliberately letting go of grudges, past hurts, put-downs, and betrayals. And embrace forgiveness. When the hurtful words and scenes pop up again in your mind, discover and practice whatever works best for you, neutralizing them and leaving them in the past where they belong. The practice of letting go and forgiving is freeing you to become more wholly your authentic self.

The mind is a negative power until you actually master it. What are all these hurts that keep popping into your awareness and sliming you? They are just past expressions of someone's negative lower mind. You can become a seasoned practitioner of forgiveness by experimenting and customizing what works best for you. Invent scenarios in your mind's eye that reenact the scene positively; practice affirmations; engage in repetition—test what facilitates your mind to let go so eventually that recurrent program of negativity is overridden and forgotten.

As a third awareness, invest time delving into concupiscence. That is, use your higher mind, your intuition to suss out the true longing of your soul. What is it that your soul yearns for, that will give it ever-joyous delight?

Various theologians have identified concupiscence with original sin. The blame is typically assigned to Adam. Poor Adam. He does not deserve that blame. Each of us committed original sin. That was early, early in the adventure when our soul was connected with the mind and first moved away from God. The bugbearish thought or act was not necessarily lust. The sinning could have been an expression of anger, greed, attachment, or ego. These are the five primary pulling-away passions to which our mind falls prey. We expressed myriad permutations as we drifted and bolted more and more into the enticements of the world, merrily sinning along, ruled increasingly by the beguilements of the senses and the demands of our ego.

The concupiscence of our soul was ever-glowing with divine longing. Our soul was and is constant in its concupiscence for God.

So, here you are again, dear friend, imprisoned in the physical, in a body with which you may have any number and kind of ongoing or newly intruding troubles, continuing your adventure of traipsing through each day, paying off and adding good debt after bad debt after so-so debt, each of which adjusts your balance sheet. Afterall, these debts are what brought you down here again and, now, no doubt, you are accumulating more debits and credits as you attempt to satisfy your lusts of the world, as noble as they might seem.

Entertain this if you will. When moved to, *remember*; invest time with true sincerity and humility and sit or lie, be still, and plumb the desire of your immaculate soul. Do your best to transcend your mind and allow the knowingness of your soul to filter through to enlighten you of its primordial timeless longing, the fulfillment of which will reward you with lasting contentment.

You will be here a while longer. Why not invest your time along with your human body, your God-given fourth beneficence, in its highest calling? That could be the best investment you make this lifetime. Regard your body as a valuable vehicle you are meant to invest. Park your body in a suitable, comfortable position on a cushion, chair, or recliner and meditate.

Even if you can be there for just two minutes, that is good and is better than not showing up. What is the best time for you when you will not be disturbed? The key is to meditate daily and be punctual to inculcate the habit. What need is there for you to reincarnate in the distant future with the possible opportunity of visiting distant galaxies and a black hole or two when, right now, you possess the vehicle for entering the most glorious worlds? You are the temple of the living God. Your spiritual senses of seeing, hearing, and traveling can be awakened and refined. You possess the vehicle, if not yet the Teacher, the method, and the mindful longing.

What is the primordial wonder of the cosmos? The Sound Current. That is the cleansing, divine Sound and Light within you, earned and experienced in the practice of daily meditation and beneficent living. What would bestow the greatest joy to your soul would be to hear the rapturous melodies and brilliant lights of the Sound Current. You may or may not presently register a whisper or a pure white buzzing of that ever-present Sound, but God is listening. When you are ripe and the time is right, your Teacher will come into your life. In the meantime, the more you invest in your spiritual concupiscence, in your ardent divine longing, the more your focus is reversed from being scattered and in thrall to the world to being devoted to a life of realizing yourself and authentic contentment.

What is contentment? It is being free and freed of desires. It is accepting and being attuned to the will of God. It is playing your part with grace and goodwill this lifetime. If your soul's and higher mind's concupiscence become so compelling that you resolve to complete your adventure in this mad, mad, mad, mad world, then your abiding contentment is in seeking a true Master, while marshalling your best discrimination, determination, and patience. If you do not feel that pull, it's fine. You have more to complete here.

Meanwhile, you can build and invest in your spiritual portfolio, which never loses value. Enjoy this human experience as best you can, ideally while maintaining an element of detachment. Being here now, knowing as best you can who you are and where and how to follow your spiritual path and pursuing it with a trusting heart—that is what can bestow fulfilling contentment. You are building a foundation, abetting your spiritual portfolio that, over time, will yield true riches.

A spiritual life, lived day after day in your own circumstances, will pay dividends. You may appreciate some of the dividends at times in your daily life, and you may not realize and experience others for years. Do your best to quiet your mind's insistence for results. You may have results. You may experience transcendent highs, see scintillating sights within. The more devotedly and actively you pursue your spiritual path, the more you need to be aware of and manage your spiritual ego. It can be deadly and deaden your progress. If you are given and enjoy a mystical experience, treasure it for the treasure it is. Rather than broadcast it, keep it to yourself. Giving your spiritual ego free rein and reign, heedless of its potential hurt and damage to you and others, will result in the recall of the dividends paying into your life and reinvesting in your spiritual portfolio.

Continue your good investments in your unique spiritual life. The contentment dividend can be both experienced and kept hidden for your benefit. The contentment dividend is earned and enjoyed by living an honest life, being kind, finding and enjoying your place in God, and investing in the four beneficences. This is building your treasure. If you take one step toward God, that Power, that LoveSource will take ten— nay, one hundred steps—toward you.

By leading a good spiritual life, true to who you are, you are transmuting yourself, becoming increasingly receptive to receiving the God-given grace that is always available. It will not change your life's trajectory. You have a script to play out. But in being receptive, humble, unassuming, grace will be showered within you and you can go through whatever life brings with an inner acceptance and contentment.

Throughout your trials and travails, your efforts and misses, you are becoming spiritually mature. Your spiritual efforts are automatically accruing and reinvesting dividends while you continue your endeavors to be and realize your best spiritual self. As you detach from the ephemeral false distractions of the without and reside more in the within, cherishing your connection, the actual answer to your hopes and dreams is being realized. That is ultimately the original Wonder, an eternal treasure of contentment that is your return to LoveSource.

About the Author

Michael Goddart, MFA, writes to empower people to lead a life of increasing awareness, bliss, and love and to realize their true self. *The Contentment Dividend* is his fifth book. His previous book, *A New Now*, won six book awards and seven honors, including the Nautilus Book Award. *In Search of Lost Lives* earned four book awards, including the National Indie Excellence Award. In this unique memoir, the 88 past lives he recovered in vivid detail illustrate his spiritual evolution. He is also the author of *BLISS: 33 Simple Ways to Awaken Further* and *Spiritual Revolution: A Seeker's Guide*, which the Hollywood Spiritual Film and Entertainment Festival named Best Spirituality/Self-Help Book. Australia's leading spiritual bookshop named *Spiritual Revolution* one of the ten greatest metaphysical books ever written.

Michael started actively searching for the truth about death and how to attain true immortality with everlasting bliss when he was 10 years old. He began daily meditation at age 19, and at 21 began to meditate for two and a half hours daily.

His spiritual quest, along with his work as an international tax consultant, has taken him to over fifty countries. Since 1974, he has journeyed thirteen times to India and also numerous times to England, Greece, Canada, Spain, and within the United States to be with those rare Teachers whom he considers to be fully realized humans.

Michael earned his MFA in creative writing at Bowling Green State University in Ohio. He currently lives in Southern California, where he loves the brilliance of the light, reading fine novels, and playing with his White Swiss Shepherd.

Kindly visit www.goddart.com for interviews, excerpts, endorsements, and more.

Milton Keynes UK
Ingram Content Group UK Ltd.
UKHW011130110624
443875UK00002B/7

9 781960 090416